Vocabulary Boosters

Workbook 2

Susan Rogers

Grass Roots Press

Edmonton, Alberta, Canada
2005

Vocabulary Boosters - Workbook 2 © 2005 Grass Roots Press

Vocabulary Boosters – Workbook 2 is published by

Grass Roots Press
A division of Literacy Services of Canada Ltd.
www.grassrootsbooks.net

AUTHOR	Susan Rogers
EDITORS	Pat Campbell, Leslie Dawson
COPY EDITOR	Judith Tomlinson
DESIGN	Lara Minja - Lime Design
LAYOUT	Debra Holstein
IMAGE RESEARCH	Kalin Jensen

ACKNOWLEDGEMENTS

We acknowledge the financial support of the Government of Canada through the Book Publishing Industry Development Program (BPIDP) for our publishing activities.

We acknowledge the support of the Alberta Foundation for the Arts for our publishing programs.

Library and Archives Canada Cataloguing in Publication

Rogers, Susan, 1952-

Vocabulary boosters / Susan Rogers.

ISBN 1-894593-40-5 (bk. 1).--ISBN 1-894593-41-3 (bk. 2).--ISBN 1-894593-42-1 (bk. 3)

1. Vocabulary--Problems, exercises, etc. 2. Readers (Adult)

3. Readers for new literates. I. Title.

PE1449.R635 2006   428.1   C2005-904172-2

Printed in Canada

Contents

About this workbook

This workbook aims to help adult learners develop their vocabulary through reading passages written at an appropriate level. The workbook is organized around four themes: health, wildlife, the environment, and popular culture. Each lesson presents a non-fiction passage that relates to one of the four themes and a set of activities. The workbook activities can be completed independently, with a tutor, or with a group.

In the pre-reading activity, the learner activates his/her prior knowledge about the reading passage by listing what he/she knows about the reading topic. Then, the learner generates questions about what he/she would like to learn about the topic; this sets a purpose for reading. After reading the passage, the learner can reflect upon the reading selection and what he/she has learned.

After completing the pre-reading activity, learners can use the glossary to enhance their understanding of the six vocabulary words that will be introduced in the passage. This is an optional activity. Repetition is essential for vocabulary development; consequently, each lesson presents the following five activities that focus on the new words:

Activity A
Each sentence provides context clues, enabling the learner to figure out the meaning of the new vocabulary words.

Activity B
The learner is required to make an inference in order to complete a sentence. This means that the learner needs to combine his/her background knowledge, vocabulary knowledge, and information from the text.

Activity C
The learner is encouraged to use meaning cues to restore deleted words from a piece of text.

Activity D
The learner engages in a writing activity, which is a useful means of vocabulary development because it makes the learner focus on words in ways that are different when he/she is reading or listening.

Activity E
This exercise provides multiple ways to extend the learner's understanding of the new vocabulary words.

This workbook also includes the following four features:
   A glossary.
   An answer key.
   Five crossword puzzles and
   word searches.
   Twenty idioms.

In addition to improving vocabulary, the workbook will provide learners with entertaining and informative passages that will help to develop reading fluency.

Lesson 1

Understanding Stress

Pre-reading Activity

What do you KNOW about stress?	What do you WANT to learn about stress?	What did you LEARN about stress?*

* Complete this column after you read the passage on the next page.

Photo: Rob Friedman

Vocabulary words

tense	pump	optimistic
anxiety	conclusion	practice

Understanding Stress

When animals are in danger, they react by fighting or running away. We respond to a threat or challenge in a similar way. Our reaction is called the "fight-or-flight" response. This is our response to stress.

When we feel stressed, our bodies release a hormone called adrenaline. This hormone causes our muscles to **tense**, our heart rate to increase, and our blood pressure to rise. These physical changes help us to defend ourselves from danger.

If the threat requires us to fight or run, we burn up the adrenaline quickly. The trouble is, most stressful events don't require us to fight or run away. So, we don't burn up all the adrenaline.

The result is a constant build-up of adrenaline in the body. This can make us feel tired. Our muscles ache. It can be hard to sleep. Some people become depressed if the stress continues. Others suffer from **anxiety**, headaches, or backaches. The long lasting effects of stress can result in serious illnesses such as heart disease and strokes.

It's all too easy to worry about things. Alarming thoughts increase our stress. They **pump** more adrenaline into our bodies when we don't need it.

You can change the way you respond to stressful events. Imagine that you go to work one day and your boss gives you an angry look. If you jump to the **conclusion** that she is angry with you, you will feel more stress. Your stress level may build up even more if you think you are about to lose your job. You can, however, change your thoughts. You can tell yourself that the boss's bad mood has nothing to do with you.

When you feel stressed, don't jump to conclusions. The worst possible outcome is not always the most likely. You can lower your stress level by controlling your thoughts. One way to do this is to turn your attention *away* from negative thoughts. Learn to replace negative thoughts with **optimistic** ones. This will calm you and help you handle stress. It won't happen overnight, but with **practice**, you may be able to change the way you respond to stress.

Discussion

Do you think that we can control our response to stress?

Why or why not?

Check your understanding

 Circle the best meaning for each bold-faced word. Try to figure out what the word means by looking at the way it is used in the sentence.

1. When you are angry, your body may feel **tense** and tight.
   a. relaxed
   b. stressed
   c. fearful

2. It's normal to feel **anxiety** before a stressful event.
   a. worry
   b. calm
   c. happiness

3. Your heart will **pump** blood through your body.
   a. stop
   b. push (circulate)
   c. skip

4. If someone is in a bad mood, we may jump to the **conclusion** that it is our fault.
   a. a request
   b. a weakness
   c. a final decision

5. I'm **optimistic** that I will find my wallet before the end of the day.
   a. feeling that things will turn out well
   b. feeling bad about something
   c. not able to see clearly

6. Hockey players **practice** for many hours each week.
   a. do something over and over again
   b. do something once
   c. never do something

Apply your understanding

 Write sentences using the vocabulary words.

tense _____

_____

anxiety _____

_____

pump _____

_____

conclusion _____

_____

optimistic _____

_____

practice _____

_____

Extend your understanding

A prefix is a part of the word that comes before the root word. A prefix has its own meaning. The prefix can help you understand what the word means.

Many words begin with the letters **re**. In some of these words **re** is a prefix. The prefix **re** means **back** or **again**.

Examples: Repay means to pay back. Retell means to tell again.

 Circle the words that start with the prefix **re** and write their meanings.

Hint: Look for the words that are made from the prefix **re** and a root word.

reappear _____

reason _____

rest _____

regain _____

recipe _____

refund _____

refill _____

red _____

replace _____

ready _____

recall _____

read _____

rebuild _____

Lesson 2

The Black Widow Spider

Pre-reading Activity

What do you KNOW about black widow spiders?	What do you WANT to learn about black widow spiders?	What did you LEARN about black widow spiders?*

* Complete this column after you read the passage on the next page.

Photo:Jon Sharp

Vocabulary words

venom	preys	numb
debris	puncture	resistant

The Black Widow Spider

Black widow spiders are one of the most deadly spiders in North America. Their **venom** is 15 times more poisonous than rattlesnake venom. Luckily, the small creatures are shy and hardly ever bite humans. In fact, the male spiders never bite.

It's easy to identify black widow spiders. They have a red spot under their round, shiny black bellies. Females are 1.5 inches (3.8 cm) long. The males, which are harmless, measure half the females' size. Baby black widow spiders are white.

Black widow spiders make webs that look like spun cotton candy. Their oddly shaped webs are stronger than any other spiders' web. The black widow spider spins her web in woodpiles and under rocks, porches, plants, or **debris**. Sometimes, the spider spins a web under the seat in outdoor toilets! The female black widow spider does not usually leave her web.

Like most spiders, the black widow **preys** on insects. When an insect gets trapped in her web, the spider makes a small **puncture** in the insect's body. Then, she sucks out the contents.

Male black widow spiders have one purpose in life: to mate. After mating, the female sometimes kills and eats the male. The female lays several batches of eggs in one summer. Each egg sac contains about 750 eggs. Normally, just one to 12 young spiders survive. The female eats the rest.

Black widow spiders may seek shelter in buildings during cold or dry weather. Sometimes, they hide in shoes or clothing. They bite when touched or squeezed, or when people disturb their web. Their bite may be sharp and painful. The poison can cause a stomach ache and sore muscles. Other symptoms include a **numb** feeling, sweating, dry mouth, and swollen eyelids. The bite is seldom fatal, but go to the doctor if you are bitten.

To control black widows, carefully clean up debris in areas where they might hide. Knock down webs with a stick and crush egg sacs and spiders. Black widow spiders are **resistant** to most insect sprays.

Discussion

Why do you think some people are afraid of spiders?

Check your understanding

 Circle the best meaning for each bold-faced word. Try to figure out what the word means by looking at the way it is used in the sentence.

1. We fear animals that have **venom** because their bite can make us sick or kill us.
   a. claws
   b. teeth
   c. poison

2. They cleaned up the **debris** to make the park safer and cleaner.
   a. flowers
   b. junk
   c. soil

3. A shark **preys** on fish because they are its main source of food.
   a. hunts
   b. prays
   c. looks at

4. If a bicycle tire gets a **puncture,** the air will escape.
   a. scratch
   b. a hole
   c. a rub

5. Before a dentist drills into your tooth, she will freeze your gum to make it **numb.**
   a. an itchy feeling
   b. no feeling
   c. a hot feeling

6. Cockroaches are **resistant** to most sprays, so they are hard to kill.
   a. killed by
   b. bigger than
   c. not affected by

Boost your understanding

 Circle the answer that makes the most sense.

1. Animals that have **venom** are dangerous because
   a. they bite you more quickly than animals that don't have venom.
   b. they can put poison into your body.
   c. venom makes an animal hungry.

2. A yard with a lot of **debris** in it is likely to look
   a. pretty.
   b. messy.
   c. empty.

3. Animals **prey** on other animals because they are
   a. looking for a mate.
   b. looking for food.
   c. looking for a hiding spot.

4. A **puncture** in a ball would cause
   a. the ball to explode.
   b. the air to leak out of the ball.
   c. the air to expand in the ball.

5. If you sit cross-legged for a long time, your legs may go **numb**. Your legs will
   a. have no feeling in them.
   b. feel very cold.
   c. feel normal.

6. If you are **resistant** to the flu
   a. you will catch the flu.
   b. you will not catch the flu.
   c. you may or may not catch the flu.

Expand your understanding

C Complete each sentence by writing the correct vocabulary word in the space.

Vocabulary words

| venom | preys | numb |
| debris | puncture | resistant |

---

1. Rats and other unwanted creatures often live in _____.

2. Tom felt _____ with shock when he heard the bad news.

3. If you _____ a balloon, it will make a loud pop.

4. Some frogs have _____ in their spit.

5. A virus can be _____ to drugs.

6. A wolf _____ on deer and rabbits.

"gives me the creeps"

A big spider "gives me the creeps."

When something "gives you the creeps," it causes you to feel scared or uncomfortable.

Apply your understanding

 Write sentences using the vocabulary words.

resistant _____

_____

puncture _____

_____

venom _____

_____

preys _____

_____

numb _____

_____

debris _____

_____

Extend your understanding

A synonym is a word that has the same meaning, or nearly the same meaning, as another word.

Debris has many synonyms. Trash is one synonym for debris.

 Circle the words below that are synonyms for **debris**.

waste	paper	bottles	garbage	plastic
rubbish	fragments	dirt	rubble	remains

Find a synonym for these words by looking in the passage about black widow spiders. Then write each synonym beside the word.

1. hunts _____

2. poison _____

3. immune _____

4. hole _____

5. frozen _____

Lesson 3

Mount St. Helens

Pre-reading Activity

What do you KNOW about Mount St. Helens?	What do you WANT to learn about Mount St. Helens?	What did you LEARN about Mount St. Helens?*

* Complete this column after you read the passage on the next page.

Vocabulary words

| eruption | bulged | lava |
| pressure | triggered | swept |

Mount St. Helens

Mount St. Helens lies asleep—for now—in the northwest United States. It is an active volcano that is famous for a huge **eruption** in 1980.

The event began in March when small earthquakes shook the mountain for two months. **Pressure** built up inside the mountain, and its north side **bulged** out. Then, on May 18, a large earthquake **triggered** the volcanic eruption.

On that day, the entire top of the mountain blew off! It sent a cloud of ash 14.8 miles (24 km) into the sky. Ash and **lava** poured out for nine hours. Strong winds blew the ash eastwards. Within three days, the ash reached the east coast of the United States.

The blast destroyed the north side of the mountain. Hot ash melted snow and ice on top of the mountain. A mixture of mud and rocks flowed down the mountain's slopes. It **swept** across the landscape. Along the way, mud and rocks destroyed trees, houses, and bridges. The slide stopped 70 miles (112 km) from the volcano.

Explosions shook the air and sent rocks, ash, and gas across the land. The hot blasts traveled at enormous speed—620 miles (998 km) per hour. The blasts burned everything in their path.

The ash, mudslides, and explosions destroyed everything they touched, changing the landscape. Millions of trees were swept away. The mountain lost 1000 feet (305 m) in height. Rock and ash filled lakes and rivers. Within months, the lava hardened to form a landscape of rock.

The eruption killed 57 people who were camping or working in the area. Many of their bodies were never found. About 200 bears, thousands of deer and elk, and millions of fish and birds died.

Mount St. Helens remains an active volcano. Geologists watch it carefully because it could erupt again one day.

Discussion
How do you think the eruption changed life around Mount St. Helens?

Check your understanding

 Circle the best meaning for each bold-faced word. Try to figure out what the word means by looking at the way it is used in the sentence.

1. During a volcanic **eruption,** hot lava comes out of the mountain.
   a. something bursting out
   b. something giving way
   c. something caving in

2. The **pressure** inside a volcano has the power to cause an eruption.
   a. explosion
   b. steam and gas
   c. force that pushes

3. Sandy's stomach **bulged** after he ate six doughnuts.
   a. blew up
   b. got smaller
   c. got bigger

4. Roberto insulted Jose, and this **triggered** an argument that ended their friendship.
   a. caused
   b. stopped
   c. delayed

5. **Lava** flows out of an active volcano and hardens into rock.
   a. ash
   b. hot liquid
   c. steam

6. Wind **swept** across the city streets, blowing garbage in the air.
   a. moved slowly
   b. moved quickly
   c. stayed still

Boost your understanding

 Circle the answer that makes the most sense.

1. The **eruption**
   a. did not cause any damage.
   b. could be heard miles away.
   c. could not be heard.

2. To enter some buildings, you must use a lot of **pressure** to open the doors. That's because
   a. some doors open automatically.
   b. some doors are locked.
   c. some doors are very heavy.

3. The suitcase **bulged** out because
   a. it had very few clothes in it.
   b. it was stuffed full of clothes.
   c. it was a brand new suitcase.

4. When a mother told her child to stop eating candy, she **triggered**
   a. a temper tantrum.
   b. a nap.
   c. a smile.

5. **Lava** could be described as
   a. a river of ice.
   b. a river of fire.
   c. a river of mud.

6. Fire **swept** through a building, which means
   a. the fire stayed on the ground level.
   b. the fire moved slowly from floor to floor.
   c. the fire traveled very fast throughout the building.

Expand your understanding

C Complete each sentence by writing the correct vocabulary word in the space.

Vocabulary words

eruption	bulged	lava
pressure	triggered	swept

---

1. The nurse applied _____ to the wound to stop the bleeding.

2. When the boss lost his temper, the room shook like a volcanic _____.

3. On volcanic mountains, you can see rocks made from _____.

4. Heavy rain turned soil into mud and _____ a landslide.

5. The raft was _____ down the river by the fast current.

6. Sandy's wallet _____ with cash after he got paid.

"swept off your feet"

Ali's charming personality "swept Tricia off her feet."

If someone "sweeps you off your feet", it means that he or she has impressed you. You may even be falling in love with him or her.

Apply your understanding

 D Write sentences using the vocabulary words.

lava _____

_____

eruption _____

_____

bulged _____

_____

pressure _____

_____

triggered _____

_____

swept _____

_____

Extend your understanding

Homophones are words that sound alike. However, they are spelled differently and have different meanings. For example, **deer** is a homophone because it sounds like **dear**. Can you find the two other homophones in the following sentence?

About 200 bears, thousands of deer and elk, and millions of fish and birds died.

The homophones are **bears,** which sounds the same as **bares** and **died**, which sounds the same as **dyed**.

(E) Can you think of some other homophones?

_____   _____

_____   _____

_____   _____

Lesson 4

Bread

Pre-reading Activity

What do you KNOW about bread?	What do you WANT to learn about bread?	What did you LEARN about bread?*

* Complete this column after you read the passage on the next page.

Photo: Edyta Powlowska

Vocabulary words

staple	overthrow	Prairies
ancient	hospitality	significant

Bread

Nothing smells more delicious than fresh-baked bread. It satisfies our hunger like no other food. Bread is a **staple** food. That's because it's cheap and handy. Bread remains a staple food, despite fad diets that promote eating fewer carbohydrates.

Bread is so common we often take it for granted. The variety of breads is endless. You might eat pita, bagels, or whole wheat bread. Your neighbour might like sourdough, rye, or white bread. Yet, all bread starts in the bakery as a mixture of flour, water, and yeast.

People began making bread in **ancient** times. The ancient Romans ate a lot of bread. Their government actually gave free grain to people living in Rome. Later, the government even baked the bread! A Roman governor once said, "Give the people bread and circuses." He believed that if you kept people well fed and happy, they would not **overthrow** the government.

Language reflects a culture's values. This is especially true of words about bread. In Arabic, the words for "bread" and "life" are almost the same. In Russia, the word for **"hospitality"** translates into "bread and salt." In North America, we use the word 'bread' in many ways. For example, the **Prairies** are called the "bread basket of the world." This is because wheat is the main crop in the Prairies. The words "bread" and "dough" are slang for money. Saying "I'm short of dough" means that you don't have enough money. A "breadwinner" is the family member who earns the most money. The phrase, "bread and butter" refers to the work you do that earns most of your money. Sometimes, we say something is "the greatest thing since sliced bread." The many uses of the word "bread" show how highly cultures value bread.

For many people, bread is an important part of every meal. Bread also plays a **significant** role in many religious ceremonies. Since bread feeds our souls as well as our stomachs, it is often called the "staff of life."

Discussion

What do you think the sentence "Give the people bread and circuses" means?

Check your understanding

 Circle the best meaning for each bold-faced word. Try to figure out what the word means by looking at the way it is used in the sentence.

1. **Staple** foods, such as bread, are an important part of a person's diet.
   a. expensive
   b. main
   c. not eaten often

2. In **ancient** times, people cooked bread over a fire.
   a. long ago
   b. new
   c. present-day

3. The people wanted to **overthrow** the government and remove it from power.
   a. elect
   b. defeat
   c. dislike

4. A kind person gives **hospitality** to strangers and friends.
   a. verbal abuse
   b. a hospital
   c. a friendly welcome

5. Grain grows well in the **Prairies** because the land is flat and treeless.
   a. a large area of mostly farmland
   b. a large area of houses
   c. a land of mountains and wild animals

6. Celebrating a birthday is a **significant** event for most people.
   a. not important
   b. something that is trivial
   c. important and full of meaning

Boost your understanding

 Circle the answer that makes the most sense.

1. We depend on **staple** foods and we eat them often. Which of the following is *not* a staple food?
   a. potatoes
   b. maple syrup
   c. bread

2. An **ancient** piece of pottery would have been made
   a. sometime in the future.
   b. thousands of years ago.
   c. yesterday.

3. If an army was **overthrown**, what happened?
   a. The army won the battle.
   b. The army was defeated.
   c. The army retreated.

4. An example of **hospitality** would be
   a. giving a friend coffee and cake.
   b. telling a friend about a good film.
   c. giving a friend some advice.

5. The **Prairies** are a good place to grow wheat because
   a. they are near the sea.
   b. they are flat and treeless.
   c. they are hard to find on a map.

6. A **significant** event in your life would be
   a. getting your first job.
   b. having a shower in the morning.
   c. getting into bed at night.

Expand your understanding

C Complete each sentence by writing the correct vocabulary word in the space.

> ## Vocabulary words
>
> staple   overthrow   Prairies
>
> ancient   hospitality   significant

1. In some countries, people _____ the government because they want a better life.

2. Driving across the _____ can be boring because the land is so flat.

3. The corner store sells _____ food, candy, and pop.

4. If you work in the _____ industry, you will help many tourists.

5. The scientist made a _____ discovery that could help people with AIDS.

6. Learning about _____ cultures is interesting.

"you're toast"

"If you touch my chocolate cake, 'you're toast,'" said Polly.

You can warn someone not to do something by using the expression "You're toast."

Apply your understanding

(D) Write sentences using the vocabulary words.

staple _____

_____

overthrow _____

_____

ancient _____

_____

hospitality _____

_____

Prairies _____

_____

significant _____

_____

Extend your understanding

A compound word is made by joining together two smaller words.

Overthrow is an example of a compound word that joins the two words **over** and **throw**.

Thinking about the two words that make up a compound word can help you understand the meaning. For example, wristwatch is a watch you wear on your wrist.

 Circle the compound words. Then write the meaning of each compound word. The first one has been done for you.

backyard   swimmer   speaker   building   jellyfish   newspaper
daylight   machine   timetable   handmade   together   underground

Compound Word	Meaning
1. backyard	a yard at the back of a house
2. _____	_____
3. _____	_____
4. _____	_____
5. _____	_____
6. _____	_____
7. _____	_____

Crossword Puzzle 1

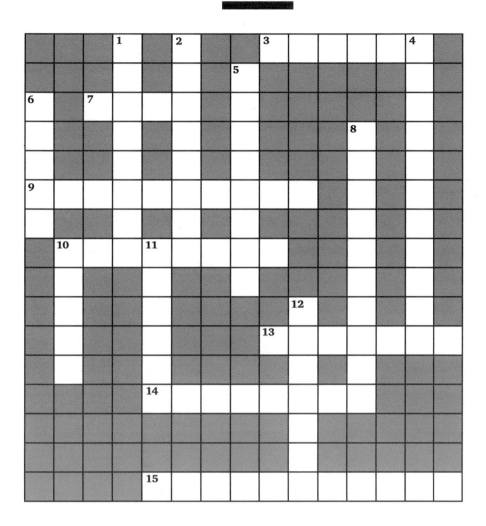

ACROSS

3. A synonym for garbage
7. Flows out of a volcano
9. Feeling positive
10. A steady force
13. Too much worry leads to this.
14. Something that happens at an active volcano
15. A good thing to offer friends

DOWN

1. If you want to learn a skill, you must do this.
2. Treeless and flat grassland
4. Important
5. To make a hole
6. Snake poison
8. A final decision
10. A hunting tiger ____ on animals.
11. Bread is a ____ food.
12. Very old

Wordsearch 1

N	S	E	P	S	I	R	B	E	D	I	S	C	E	O
H	O	S	P	I	T	A	L	I	T	Y	E	E	N	O
A	I	F	G	G	E	L	P	A	T	S	I	T	P	I
N	C	E	U	N	C	S	Y	E	R	P	R	T	E	P
C	L	N	F	I	M	O	N	E	V	O	I	N	E	I
I	E	U	I	F	A	T	N	L	S	M	A	E	M	O
E	E	B	C	I	U	N	A	C	I	P	R	R	I	P
N	T	I	P	C	E	V	X	S	L	U	P	R	P	I
T	I	M	T	A	A	C	T	I	S	U	T	I	C	E
E	L	E	S	N	A	I	I	S	E	R	S	I	P	U
N	A	Y	N	T	C	L	E	T	A	T	A	I	A	P
N	O	I	T	P	U	R	E	A	C	I	Y	O	O	E
C	U	P	S	A	P	E	I	T	E	A	E	T	B	N
R	I	E	E	I	T	A	R	E	T	O	R	A	M	E
C	E	C	P	U	N	C	T	U	R	E	N	P	P	P

The letters in the word search puzzle form words. Circle the words listed below in the word search puzzle. The words are horizontal, vertical, diagonal, and backwards.

ancient	practice
anxiety	Prairies
conclusion	pressure
debris	preys
eruption	puncture
hospitality	significant
lava	staple
optimistic	venom

Lesson 5

Shift Work

Pre-reading Activity

What do you KNOW about shift work?	What do you WANT to learn about shift work?	What did you LEARN about shift work?*

* Complete this column after you read the passage on the next page.

Photo: Richard Stouffer

Vocabulary words

essential	restores	alert
alter	function	activates

Shift Work

More than 22 million people in North America are shift workers. They work in many places, such as hospitals and factories. Shift workers also build bridges and highways. Society depends on the **essential** services they provide.

There are two types of shift work. Some people always work the night shift. Other people work two or three different shifts. For example, they might work from 7 a.m. to 3 p.m. for two weeks. Then, their next two-week shift might be from 3 p.m. to 11 p.m.

The body operates on a 24-hour sleep-wake cycle. Something like an internal clock regulates this cycle. This clock follows Nature's cycle of day and night. We are all programmed to sleep when it's dark and to wake when it's light.

It takes our bodies several days to adjust to a new time schedule. After working a few nights, many shift workers must change back to day shift. When that happens, they have to set their internal clock back to "normal." Because shift workers **alter** their sleep times, their sleep-wake cycle is disturbed. That's why shift workers find it difficult to sleep during the day, even though they are tired.

Sleep is essential to good health, but many shift workers suffer from lack of sleep. Sleep rests and **restores** our bodies so that we can **function** properly. Shift workers often struggle to stay **alert** on the job. In fact, 20 percent of shift workers report falling asleep at work.

There's no easy solution to getting a good sleep. The best way is to help the body adjust to daytime sleep. For instance, sunlight **activates** the daytime clock. So, some shift workers find that it helps to wear dark glasses on the way home. This gets their bodies ready for sleep. Shift workers need dark, quiet rooms for sleep. They should also keep to a regular sleep schedule, even if this means daytime sleeping on nights off. At home, they learn to adjust the day's schedule. They change mealtimes and other activities to fit their sleep-wake cycle.

Some workers succeed at working night shifts. Usually, this means they put extra effort into managing their lives. More people will probably face the challenge of shift work in the future.

Discussion

Why do you think the number of shift workers will increase in the future?

Check your understanding

 Circle the best meaning for each bold-faced word. Try to figure out what the word means by looking at the way it is used in the sentence.

1. Nurses and bus drivers perform **essential** jobs in our society.
   a. boring
   b. necessary
   c. unnecessary

2. Working late shifts forced Ali to **alter** his habit of getting up early.
   a. expect
   b. change
   c. ask

3. Resting and eating often **restore** your energy when you feel tired.
   a. make it the way it was before
   b. make it sleepy
   c. make it hungry

4. Visitors have to bang on the door because the doorbell doesn't **function**.
   a. look good
   b. think
   c. work

5. A police officer needs to be **alert** so that she is ready to act if something happens.
   a. tired
   b. angry
   c. watchful

6. Turning on the ignition **activates** the car engine.
   a. starts it working
   b. repairs
   c. stops it from working

Boost your understanding

 Circle the answer that makes the most sense.

1. The manager said, "It is **essential** to be polite to customers." That means
   a. employees can be rude if customers are rude to them.
   b. employees must be polite at all times.
   c. employees can be polite if they feel like it.

2. If your boss **alters** your shift, he
   a. keeps you on the same shift.
   b. fires you for no reason.
   c. changes the time you start work.

3. The carpenters **restore** old houses. This means the carpenters
   a. repair and repaint houses.
   b. tear down houses.
   c. build new houses.

4. People **function** better when they are
   a. tired and hungry.
   b. rested and well fed.
   c. upset and angry.

5. You should be most **alert**
   a. just before you fall asleep.
   b. when you are crossing the road.
   c. when you are watching television.

6. A person **activates** an automatic door by
   a. stepping in front of the door.
   b. asking that the door be opened.
   c. banging on the door until it opens.

Expand your understanding

C Complete each sentence by writing the correct vocabulary word in the space.

Vocabulary words		
essential	restores	alert
alter	function	activates

1. In order to _____ properly, a car must have regular tune-ups.

2. A timer _____ the lights to turn on at 7 a.m.

3. A fire alarm will _____ you to a fire in the building.

4. My sister wants me to _____ her skirt by shortening it.

5. Mary _____ furniture so that she can sell it for a profit.

6. It's _____ for fire fighters to get to a fire quickly.

"sleepyhead"

The little boy yawned. His father said, "It's late. Go to bed, *sleepyhead.*"

We often call a child who is tired a "sleepyhead."

Lesson 5

Apply your understanding

 Write sentences using the vocabulary words.

essential _____

_____

restores _____

_____

function _____

_____

alter _____

_____

alert _____

_____

activates _____

_____

Extend your understanding

Some words can be used as a noun or a verb. For example, the word **function** can be used as a noun or a verb. The meaning of a word changes, depending on how it is used in sentence.

In the following sentences, **function** is used as a verb.

The television will not function unless it is turned on.

If you want to rest on a hike, a log can function as a seat.

As a verb, **function** means

a. to work

b. to perform a certain use.

In the following sentences, **function** is used as a noun.

The function of a kettle is to boil water.

The mall sponsors functions such as concerts and fashion shows.

As a noun, **function** means

a. the purpose of something

b. a public event.

 Write two sentences using the word **function**. Use the word **function** as a verb in the first sentence and as a noun in the second sentence.

_____

_____

_____

_____

Lesson 6

Tigers in Trouble

Pre-reading Activity

What do you KNOW about tigers?	What do you WANT to learn about tigers?	What did you LEARN about tigers?*

* Complete this column after you read the passage on the next page.

Photo: Kevin Tate

Vocabulary words

predicted	habitat	conservation
extinct	ban	plight

Tigers in Trouble

People **predicted** that tigers would be **extinct** by 2000. Thankfully, that did not happen. Tigers still live in India, China, Indonesia, and Russia. However, tigers are in danger. Hunting and loss of **habitat** threaten their survival.

Tigers live in thick forests, jungles, grasslands, and swamps. They hunt under trees and in long grass. They catch deer, wild pigs, monkeys, and snakes. As human populations grow, people cut down forests to plant crops. The land becomes farmland. This is how tigers lose the habitat they need to survive.

When tigers are forced to live in smaller areas, they have fewer animals to hunt. In these situations, tigers sometimes attack humans. More often, they kill domestic animals such as goats and cows. Farmers protect themselves and their animals by killing tigers seen near villages.

Loss of habitat is a serious problem. However, hunting presents the main danger to tigers. Once, people hunted them for their fur. No two tigers have the same pattern of stripes. Dealers paid high prices for tiger skins. The worldwide **ban** on tiger skins stopped much of the fur trade. Although it is illegal, people still hunt tigers for bones and other body parts. The parts are used to make traditional medicines. Sometimes, hunters are caught and fined. However, the fines are not high enough to stop them from hunting.

What is being done to save tigers? Many countries have set up **conservation** areas. Farming is banned in these areas, and hunting is illegal. Wildlife officers search out hunters and try to stop the trade in tiger parts. They also encourage local people to support tiger conservation.

Setting up conservation areas has helped tigers. However, they are still in danger. Publicity about their **plight** improves their chances for survival.

Discussion

Do you think that tigers should be killed to make traditional medicine for humans? Why or why not?

Check your understanding

 Circle the best meaning for each bold-faced word. Try to figure out what the word means by looking at the way it is used in the sentence.

1. Weather experts **predicted** that the heat wave would continue for many days.
   a. made a statement about the future
   b. ignored something that has happened
   c. judged something as good or bad

2. Dinosaurs used to live on earth, but they became **extinct** millions of years ago.
   a. survived
   b. stayed around
   c. no longer surviving in this world

3. An animal's **habitat** is an area where it finds food and water.
   a. a hole where an animal lives
   b. the natural home of an animal
   c. a wire cage for animals

4. Smokers stand outside to smoke because many places have a **ban** on smoking indoors.
   a. not allow
   b. make a loud noise about something
   c. tie something down

5. People work on **conservation** projects because they care about nature.
   a. protection of plants and animals
   b. payment to see animals
   c. destruction of animals

6. The **plight** of sick children in Africa is a result of poverty, war, and disease.
   a. something light
   b. something birds do when they are afraid
   c. bad situation

Boost your understanding

 Circle the answer that makes the most sense.

1. If the weather report **predicted** rain, you should
   a. wear shorts and sandals.
   b. hang out the washing.
   c. take an umbrella.

2. The dodo bird is now **extinct**. If you want to see what a dodo bird looks like, you will have to
   a. visit a zoo to see dodo birds in cages.
   b. visit South America to see dodo birds in the wild.
   c. look at photographs of dodo birds.

3. Forest fires destroy animal **habitat**. When this happens
   a. animals lose their natural home.
   b. animals become tame.
   c. animals live on roads.

4. Some people would like to have a **ban** on hunting grizzly bears. They want
   a. to protect bears by not allowing anyone to kill them.
   b. to make it easier to hunt bears in national parks.
   c. to get rid of all dangerous bears.

5. A **conservation** area is likely to be a place where
   a. people can hunt with a license.
   b. hunting is banned.
   c. hunting is allowed.

6. News stories about the **plight** of hungry children
   a. show children buying cereal.
   b. cause people to give money to help the children.
   c. show healthy children.

Expand your understanding

C Complete each sentence by writing the correct vocabulary word in the space.

Vocabulary words

predicted	habitat	conservation
extinct	ban	plight

---

1. There is a _____ on skateboarding on city streets.

2. Low rainfall means that water _____ is necessary.

3. Panda bears are in danger of becoming _____.

4. Rosa _____ that the Yankees would win the World Series.

5. The _____ of people left homeless after the hurricane was terrible.

6. Plants grow well in a _____ that suits their needs.

"jungle mouth"

Most people have "jungle mouth" when they wake up in the morning.

To have a "jungle mouth" means that your breath smells bad.

Apply your understanding

 D Write sentences using the vocabulary words.

predicted _____

_____

ban _____

_____

extinct _____

_____

habitat _____

_____

plight _____

_____

conservation _____

_____

Extend your understanding

A prefix is a part of the word that comes before the root word. A prefix has its own meaning.

The prefix *pre* means **before**. The word, **predict** *means* to say or write about something before it happens.

 Keep in mind the meaning of *pre*, and decide whether these statements are true or false. Write T for true and F for false.

1. _____ A premature baby is born after the due date.

2. _____ If you see a preview of a film, you will see it before it is released to the general public.

3. _____ Preparing for a party means cleaning up after the event.

Lesson 7

Oil Spill at Sea

Pre-reading Activity

What do you KNOW about oil spills?	What do you WANT to learn about oil spills?	What did you LEARN about oil spills?*

* Complete this column after you read the passage on the next page.

Photo: Maritime Safety Queenskland

Vocabulary words

transport	marine	remote
reef	insulate	reduce

Oil Spill at Sea

———

The *Exxon Valdez* was an oil tanker that made history on March 24, 1989. The ship, which was built to **transport** oil, left the port of Valdez, Alaska on the evening of March 23. It had a full load of oil.

Floating ice forced the ship to change its course. The ship hit rocks on a **reef**. The crash damaged the ship's hull. More than 11 million gallons of oil leaked into the sea. This amount of oil would fill 125 Olympic-sized swimming pools. This accident damaged the environment more than any other oil spill in U.S. history.

Oil does not mix with water. Instead, it floats on the surface. Floating oil blocks sunlight and oxygen from reaching the **marine** life below. The oil also forms balls of tar that stick to sea birds. The birds cannot fly or float. Their feathers no longer **insulate** them from the cold.

Marine mammals, such as seals, try to clean oil off their bodies. They swallow oil, which poisons them. Oil spills also destroy the feeding grounds of oysters and shrimp.

The *Exxon Valdez* oil spill occurred in a **remote** area that is home to many sea animals. The oil spill took four years to clean up. Over 10,000 people and 1,000 boats helped. The cleanup ended even though many areas were still polluted. It was too difficult for workers to reach all the remote shorelines.

Workers counted more than 35,000 dead seabirds. However, most dead birds were not counted because they sunk in the sea. So, experts believe that 250,000 seabirds actually died. Experts also estimate that the oil spill killed 2,800 sea otters, 250 eagles, 22 killer whales, and billions of salmon and herring eggs.

Oil spills happen every year. Mistakes at sea cause some oil spills. Bad weather and terrorists have also caused oil spills. Until we **reduce** the amount of oil we use, oil spills will continue to pollute the ocean.

Discussion

What do you think can be done to stop oil spills in the ocean?

Check your understanding

 Circle the best meaning for each bold-faced word. Try to figure out what the word means by looking at the way it is used in the sentence.

1. Trucks **transport** fruit from farms to grocery stores.
   a. take it easy
   b. take a train to a port
   c. take people or goods from one place to another

2. Ships can sink if they hit a **reef.**
   a. large wave
   b. sand at the bottom of the sea
   c. rocks near the surface of the sea

3. Gift shops near the beach sell **marine** items such as model ships and lighthouses.
   a. having to do with the sea
   b. something to do with the farm
   c. something to do with the zoo

4. A thick coat will **insulate** you and keep you warm.
   a. cover and protect from the sun
   b. cover and protect from cold
   c. cover and protect from noise

5. To reach a **remote** area, you would have to travel some distance from a town or city.
   a. far away
   b. close by
   c. in a city

6. A good way to **reduce** your heating bill is to lower the thermostat at night.
   a. make faster
   b. make heavier
   c. make less

Boost your understanding

 Circle the answer that makes the most sense.

1. Ships, trains, and trucks **transport** goods. They
   a. carry products from one place to another.
   b. sell corn at the side of the road.
   c. store items from one season to the next season.

2. Many ships have sunk on **reefs**. If you dive near a reef, you might see
   a. submarines.
   b. shipwrecks.
   c. whales.

3. Many families visit zoos to see the **marine** animals. What animals do they want to see?
   a. tigers and lions.
   b. seals and sea otters.
   c. snakes and lizards.

4. Foam cups **insulate** hot coffee better than paper cups. Coffee in a foam cup is more likely to
   a. cool down faster.
   b. taste different.
   c. stay hot longer.

5. In the **remote** areas of Alaska, you are likely to find
   a. big supermarkets.
   b. wild animals.
   c. busy roads.

6. If you wanted to **reduce** your rent, you might look for
   a. a bigger apartment.
   b. a quieter apartment.
   c. a roommate.

Expand your understanding

 Complete each sentence by writing the correct vocabulary word in the space.

> **Vocabulary words**
>
> | transport | marine | remote |
> |-----------|--------|--------|
> | reef | insulate | reduce |

1. Thanh wants to _____ the amount of gas he uses by driving a smaller car.

2. In northern climates, builders must _____ a house from the cold.

3. Airplanes _____ people all over the world.

4. Sailors listen to the _____ weather forecast.

5. People like to dive around a _____ because fish live near the rocks.

6. Some tourists go to _____ areas of the world to get away from other tourists.

"hit rock bottom"

idiom for today

After losing his job and his wallet on the same day, Joe "hit rock bottom."

To "hit rock bottom" means to reach the lowest possible level.

Apply your understanding

 Write sentences using the vocabulary words.

transport _____

_____

reef _____

_____

remote _____

_____

insulate _____

_____

marine _____

_____

reduce _____

_____

Extend your understanding

Marine is just one word that is associated with the sea. There are many more such as **navy, sailor, and oil-tanker.**

 Work with a partner. Try to think of some other words that are associated with the sea. We have given you some prompts to get you started.

Can you think of some animals that live in the sea?

Can you think of some jobs that are associated with the sea?

Can you think of weather that is associated with the sea?

Can you think of some plants you'd find in the sea?

Can you think of some sports associated with the sea?

Lesson 8

Popular Culture

Body Language

Pre-reading Activity

What do you KNOW about body language?	What do you WANT to learn about body language?	What did you LEARN about body language?*

* Complete this column after you read the passage on the next page.

Photo: Amand Rohde

Vocabulary words

contradicts	defensive	universal
reprimanded	indifference	unique

Body Language

People communicate in two ways — with words and with body language. Yet, people's words and actions don't always agree. Sometimes a person's body language **contradicts** his words. An example might be a man talking to a woman. The man's eyes look around the room while he talks to the woman. His actions show that he is not interested in the conversation.

Body language can also reveal unspoken feelings. If a person is **reprimanded** for being late, she may cross her arms. That shows she feels **defensive**. She uses body language instead of words to defend herself.

People use body language to show their emotions. They shrug their shoulders to show **indifference**. A smile shows happiness. However, it may be a false smile if it doesn't involve the eyes. You've probably seen people who smile, but their eyes look cold.

Body language can be used to take control of a conversation. For instance, have you ever watched a person nod her head during a conversation? When a listener nods her head quickly, it sends a message to the speaker. The quick nodding shows that she wants to interrupt and start talking. Nodding her head slowly would encourage the speaker to continue.

> ▶ A *gesture* is an action that you do which helps to show what you mean or feel.

If something goes wrong, people can comfort themselves with body language. Athletes often cradle their heads if they make a mistake. This *gesture* reminds us of being cradled as a baby. Hugging yourself or stroking your arm is also a comforting gesture.

People use body language to communicate things they won't put into words. Patting someone on the back during a hug is not always a sign of affection. Sometimes, it's a sign that the person wants to pull away from the hug.

Understanding body language is tricky. Not all cultures use body language the same way. In North America, raising your eyebrows indicates surprise. In Japan, it's a sign of rudeness. However, some gestures, such as a smile, are **universal**.

Paying close attention to body language can help you communicate better. Every person has his or her own **unique** gestures. You need to study people's words and actions carefully to understand their body language.

Discussion

What type of body language do you use to show your emotions?

For example, what do you do when you feel bored?

Check your understanding

 Circle the best meaning for each bold-faced word. Try to figure out what the word means by looking at the way it is used in the sentence.

1. Rosa claims to like Pedro, but she **contradicts** this by saying he is boring.
   a. agreeing
   b. saying the opposite
   c. being confused

2. Children are often **reprimanded** by teachers for not doing their homework.
   a. told they have done something wrong
   b. asked for help
   c. praised for a job well done

3. Lee's attitude becomes **defensive** when his coach yells at him.
   a. self-protective
   b. hurtful to someone
   c. continuing to do something

4. The players' **indifference** showed that they had lost interest in the game.
   a. being different
   b. caring too much about something
   c. not caring about something

5. All cultures believe in love. It is a **universal** feeling.
   a. somewhere
   b. nowhere
   c. everywhere

6. Steve has a **unique** opportunity to sing for the Pope.
   a. the same as many
   b. dangerous
   c. one of a kind

Boost your understanding

 Circle the answer that makes the most sense.

1. A person who **contradicts** you all the time is likely to be
   a. funny.
   b. annoying.
   c. stupid.

2. When a child is **reprimanded**, he might
   a. feel upset at being scolded.
   b. feel happy to get praised.
   c. look forward to getting more reprimands.

3. People with a **defensive** attitude
   a. learn from their mistakes.
   b. reject criticism.
   c. are willing to listen.

4. If you show **indifference** about winning or losing a game, it means
   a. that you care about winning.
   b. that you can't make up your mind.
   c. that you don't care whether you win or lose.

5. A **universal** way to greet visitors is to
   a. expect them to give presents.
   b. offer them food or a drink.
   c. ask them to tidy the house.

6. If you ask the hairdresser for a **unique** hairstyle, you will get
   a. a hairstyle that nobody else has.
   b. the most popular hairstyle.
   c. a hairstyle from a book.

Expand your understanding

 Complete each sentence by writing the correct vocabulary word in the space.

Vocabulary words

contradicts	defensive	universal
reprimanded	indifference	unique

---

1. His father _____ him for losing his wallet.

2. Some actors are liked by everyone. They have _____ attraction.

3. Nancy made a _____ wedding dress from old curtains.

4. When Nat says his room is tidy, his mother always _____ him.

5. Denzil's _____ to getting a job upset his wife.

6. Eva was very _____ when her friend asked why she needed to borrow money.

"on the same wavelength"

idiom for today

Andy and Fatima are "on the same wavelength." They both like action movies and popcorn.

If you are "on the same wavelength," it means you agree and have similar opinions.

Another idiom, **"see eye to eye"** means the same as "on the same wavelength."

Apply your understanding

 Write sentences using the vocabulary words.

contradicts _____

_____

reprimanded _____

_____

defensive _____

_____

indifference _____

_____

unique _____

_____

universal _____

_____

Extend your understanding

Two words in the passage have **uni** at the beginning—**uni**que and **uni**versal.

Uni means one. It is used in many common words.
- **unite** means to bring together as one.
- **union** means to join together as one.
- **unify** means to make into one.

Here are some words that begin with *uni*. The meaning of each word has something to do with the number one. Complete each sentence by choosing a word from the list. You may wish to look up the meanings in a dictionary.

unicorns   uniform   union   united   university

1. Police officers and soldiers wear a _____.

2. Students go to a _____ to get degrees in science and other subjects.

3. People who believe in the same thing are _____ in their beliefs.

4. Children like to read about _____. They are made-up creatures that look like a horse with one long straight horn.

5. Marriage is sometimes called a _____ between two people.

Crossword Puzzle 2

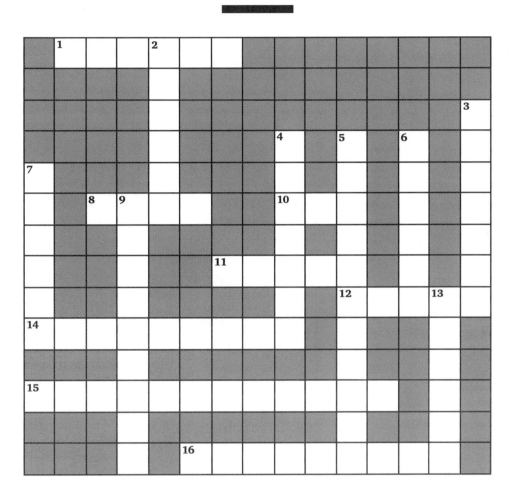

ACROSS

1. Make smaller
8. A group of rocks near the surface of the sea
10. To forbid or not allow
11. To change something
12. Watchful and ready to take action
14. To carry across land or sea
15. Lack of interest
16. Self-protective attitude

DOWN

2. One of a kind
3. No longer surviving in the world
4. Natural home of an animal
5. The opposite of agrees
6. Something to do with the sea.
7. A bad situation
9. Necessary
13. A faraway place

Wordsearch 2

C	L	A	I	T	N	E	S	S	E	R	I	R	A	E
O	T	R	O	P	S	N	A	R	T	T	A	L	T	N
N	D	R	A	D	T	C	N	I	T	X	E	O	H	L
T	E	R	A	R	E	D	U	C	E	R	M	A	G	T
R	I	R	L	T	E	F	U	E	T	E	B	E	I	R
A	T	T	M	L	S	E	A	R	I	T	P	L	R
D	A	E	E	I	M	P	V	N	T	M	L	I	P	A
I	C	E	E	T	E	E	N	A	S	F	E	A	E	L
C	U	T	R	I	A	N	T	L	I	I	T	A	R	T
T	F	N	E	E	N	O	I	T	T	E	V	N	M	E
S	I	E	I	E	A	C	A	R	T	T	X	E	E	R
T	L	S	E	Q	B	F	I	R	A	R	R	L	I	D
T	E	E	S	R	U	S	A	T	R	M	S	T	F	E
I	N	D	I	F	F	E	R	E	N	C	E	A	T	I
C	N	B	S	D	I	E	S	E	A	A	E	F	A	I

The letters in the word search puzzle form words. Circle the words listed below in the word search puzzle. The words are horizontal, vertical, diagonal, and backwards.

alert	indifference
alter	marine
ban	plight
contradicts	reduce
defensive	reef
essential	remote
extinct	transport
habitat	unique

Lesson 9

The Problem with Snoring

Pre-reading Activity

What do you KNOW about snoring?	What do you WANT to learn about snoring?	What did you LEARN about snoring?*

* Complete this column after you read the passage on the next page.

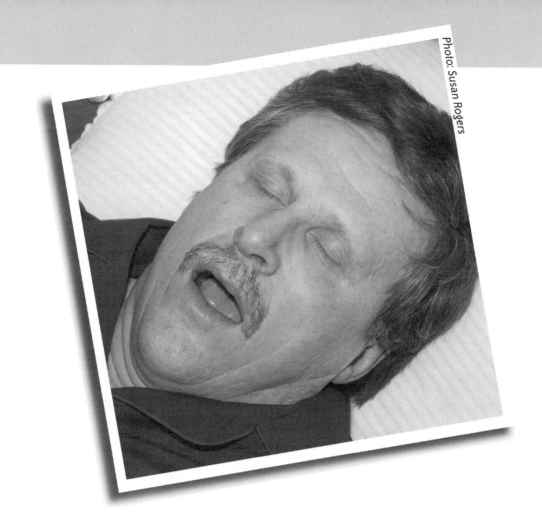

Photo: Susan Rogers

Vocabulary words

deprivation	vibrate	sag
passages	risk factors	chronic

The Problem with Snoring

At the end of a long day, drifting off to sleep feels great. However, waking up to your own grunts and snores in the middle of the night is annoying. It is also embarrassing! It's even harder to sleep when the person *beside* you is snoring.

Snoring frustrates both the sleeper and the listener. It can also be a health risk for the snorer. The problem is more than noise. Our bodies need a constant supply of oxygen. People who snore simply don't get enough air or oxygen. Snoring can also increase blood pressure. This can lead to heart disease, strokes, and heart attacks.

You might think that a person who snores is enjoying a deep sleep. But, that is not true. Snorers suffer from sleep **deprivation** because their snoring keeps waking them up. They feel sleepy the next day because they did not get enough oxygen at night. Snorers who work in high-risk jobs have a greater chance of injury when they are tired.

Snoring occurs when air cannot flow freely through air **passages** behind the mouth and nose. This causes the soft tissues behind the throat to **vibrate** and make a loud noise. Many factors limit the flow of air. For example, colds and allergies can block nasal passages. This limits airflow through the nose. If you sleep on your back, your tongue may fall backwards into your throat. This can narrow and restrict the flow of air.

One of the highest **risk factors** linked with snoring is being over age 50. Have you noticed that snoring tends to grow worse with age? This is because older people's throat muscles relax, causing the nearby tissue to **sag** and vibrate more. Being overweight is also a risk factor. The throat muscles of a large person are less firm and more likely to vibrate.

Snoring can happen to anyone. In fact, about 45 percent of adults snore from time to time while about 25 percent are **chronic** snorers. Snoring is the brunt of many jokes, but it is no laughing matter.

Discussion

What would you do if your partner had a snoring problem?

Check your understanding

 Circle the best meaning for each bold-faced word. Try to figure out what the word means by looking at the way it is used in the sentence.

1. If you suffer from sleep **deprivation,** you will be tired.
   a. not having enough
   b. not being happy
   c. not being healthy

2. If your nasal **passages** get blocked, the air does not move through them.
   a. a way through something
   b. a way over something
   c. a way under something

3. My cell phone **vibrates** when I get a call.
   a. turn around
   b. move quickly back and forth
   c. hop up and down

4. There are many **risk factors** that affect your health. For example, smoking is a risk factor for lung cancer.
   a. things that are dangerous
   b. things that make it more likely that a health problem will occur
   c. things that are not important

5. After many years, the weight of people sitting on a chair will make it **sag**.
   a. fall over
   b. make a gentle sound
   c. hang down in the middle

6. People can suffer from **chronic** back pain for many years.
   a. lasting a long time
   b. hurting a great deal
   c. making a loud noise

Boost your understanding

 B Circle the answer that makes the most sense.

1. People who suffer from food **deprivation**
   a. are healthy.
   b. are hungry.
   c. are well-fed.

2. The secret **passage** was located
   a. in the castle.
   b. in the box.
   c. in the sky.

3. People use a pad that **vibrates** on their backs because
   a. it cleans the back.
   b. it relaxes tired muscles.
   c. it stops cuts from bleeding.

4. One of the **risk factors** linked to skin cancer is
   a. sun tanning.
   b. hand cream.
   c. dry skin.

5. A bed that **sags** in the middle is
   a. the most expensive bed to buy.
   b. a good choice for two people.
   c. likely to be uncomfortable.

6. The best treatment for a **chronic** toothache is
   a. to wait and see if it gets worse.
   b. to see a dentist.
   c. to have a good night's sleep.

Expand your understanding

 Complete each sentence by writing the correct vocabulary word in the space.

Vocabulary words

deprivation	vibrate	sag
passages	risk factors	chronic

---

1. Serge is not a good baker because his cakes _____ in the centre.

2. Wild animals can suffer from food _____.

3. Lin was a _____ complainer; she was never happy.

4. Some of the _____ linked to road accidents are bad road conditions, drinking and driving, and using cell phones.

5. There was a _____ between the houses, which made it easier to get to the park.

6. Your eardrum can _____ if music is too loud.

"Let sleeping dogs lie."

idiom for today

My boss's remarks about my work made me angry, but my friend told me to "let sleeping dogs lie." My friend said I'd only make things worse if I argued with my boss.

If you are told to "let sleeping dogs lie," it means don't disturb a situation, as it would result in trouble.

Apply your understanding

 Write sentences using the vocabulary words.

deprivation _____

_____

vibrate _____

_____

passages _____

_____

risk factors _____

_____

sag _____

_____

chronic _____

_____

Extend your understanding

Some words have more than one meaning. In *The Problem with Snoring,* the word **passage** means a way through.

Passage has three other meanings:
1. a short piece of text from a book.
2. a journey by sea or air.
3. something that passes – like the passage of time.

Another example of a word with multiple meanings is **block**.
Block has three meanings:
1. to stop or make passage difficult.
2. a solid piece of material, with one or more flat sides.
3. a large building divided into apartments.

 The following words have more than one meaning. Write down as many meanings as you can for each word. Then, look up the word in your dictionary to check in your answers.

step _____

stroke _____

roll _____

point _____

note _____

Write down some other words that have more than one meaning.

_____

_____

Lesson 10

Black Bears

Pre-reading Activity

What do you KNOW about black bears?	What do you WANT to learn about black bears?	What did you LEARN about black bears?*

* Complete this column after you read the passage on the next page.

Photo:Steve Geer

Vocabulary words

| misconception | versatile | solitary |
| intrude | enables | adaptable |

Black Bears

People have a **misconception** about American black bears. We think that they are always black. But, in fact, they can range from jet black to shades of brown and blonde. Their most common colour is dark brown or black. There is even a unique population of white bears living on a remote British Columbia island.

A black bear's appetite for any kind of food can get it into trouble with humans. Black bears will **intrude** into campsites and urban areas. They will even swim to island campsites for food. They will break into homes and get into garbage. Sometimes, bears will even unscrew jar lids! They are intelligent animals with good memories and will return to places where they find food. Because of this habit, wildlife managers sometimes relocate black bears to remote areas.

Bears are **versatile** creatures with many different skills. They can run at speeds that reach 30 miles per hour (48 kph). And they can climb trees as fast as a squirrel. They are good swimmers and use their paws to fish. Their sense of smell is very sharp, which **enables** them find food in unlikely places.

American black bears are the smallest and most widespread bear in North America. Their woodland range extends from Alaska to Mexico. Over half of all North American black bears live in Canada. They are **solitary** creatures that prefer to live in forests with low human populations. However, in northern Labrador, black bears have moved to the tundra, a flat treeless land. Their **adaptable** nature means that they can live in different habitats.

More and more people are building homes in bear habitat. This means that bears and people have a higher chance of coming into contact. However, black bears usually stay away from people, because of their shy nature. They seldom attack or kill people. Yet, black bears can still be dangerous. If a human gets too close to their cubs or food source, black bears may attack.

———

Discussion

In the future, what do you think will be the greatest threat to the black bear population?

Check your understanding

 Circle the best meaning for each bold-faced word. Try to figure out what the word means by looking at the way it is used in the sentence.

1. There is a **misconception** that Canada is cold all year round.
    a. a mistake made on purpose
    b. something missed by accident
    c. wrong idea

2. A **versatile** musician will play many different musical instruments.
    a. one who hears well
    b. one with many skills
    c. cute-looking

3. **Solitary** animals such as tigers do not live in groups.
    a. alone
    b. one of a pair
    c. with babies

4. People who **intrude** into your home probably want to steal from you.
    a. stick out
    b. run away from
    c. enter without being invited

5. Rats are very **adaptable**. They are found all over the world.
    a. able to change to fit into a new situation
    b. always do things in the same way
    c. refuse to change

6. Carl's parents gave him some money, which **enables** him to start his own business.
    a. stopped him from workimg
    b. made him think hard
    c. made it possible for

Boost your understanding

 B Circle the answer that makes the most sense.

1. Mike had the **misconception** that Ramon was a good cook. Mike was surprised
   a. when Ramon cooked him a delicious meal.
   b. when Ramon cooked him a very tough steak.
   c. when Ramon wore a chef's hat.

2. A **versatile** actor would be
   a. able to play only the hero.
   b. able to play the hero and the villian.
   c. able to play only the villian.

3. A **solitary** person would prefer
   a. working on her own.
   b. working with one person.
   c. working with many people.

4. If a loud person **intrudes** on your quiet time, you might feel
   a. curious.
   b. happy.
   c. angry.

5. An **adaptable** person is likely to enjoy
   a. situations where things change often.
   b. situations where things stay the same.
   c. situations where nothing ever changes.

6. Studying every night **enables** Jamal to
   a. avoid school.
   b. pass his exams.
   c. sleep through the night.

Expand your understanding

C Complete each sentence by writing the correct vocabulary word in the space.

Vocabulary words

| misconception | versatile | solitary |
| intrude | enables | adaptable |

1. Learning to drive _____ Ali to stop taking the bus.

2. My neighbour likes to _____ when I have parties.

3. I prefer to live alone, but I'm _____ and I can live with others if necessary.

4. Win is _____; she runs the beauty shop and teaches dancing.

5. My grandfather does not like visitors because he has a _____ nature.

6. It's a _____ to think that the water in our homes is free.

"Claws are showing."

I think Sonia's "claws are showing" because her friend won the lottery.

If your "claws are showing," it means that people can tell you feel jealous or resentful about something.

Apply your understanding

 Write sentences using the vocabulary words.

misconception _____

_____

enables _____

_____

versatile _____

_____

solitary _____

_____

intrude _____

_____

adaptable _____

_____

Extend your understanding

> A prefix is a part of the word that comes before the root word. A prefix has its own meaning.

The prefix **mis** means wrong or badly. It makes a word mean the opposite, or negative, of its root word. For example:

The opposite of the root word **behave** is **misbehave**.
The opposite of the root word **deal** is **misdeal**.
The opposite of the root word **spell** is **misspell**.

The root word **conception** means an understanding or a thought. The word also means the beginning of a process as in the conception of a baby.

If you have a **misconception,** then you have a wrong understanding of something. It is very close in meaning to **misunderstanding**. They are synonyms. **Misunderstandings** happen between people. A **misconception** is usually about facts or ideas.

(E) List six words that use the prefix **mis**. Then, you can check your answers in the dictionary.

_____   _____   _____

_____   _____   _____

Lesson 11

Antarctica

Pre-reading Activity

What do you KNOW about the Antarctica?	What do you WANT to learn about the Antarctica?	What did you LEARN about the Antarctica?*

* Complete this column after you read the passage on the next page.

Photo: Vera Boğaerts

Vocabulary words

| interior | hardy | permanent |
| harsh | abundant | dispose |

Antarctica

Antarctica is a unique continent that lies over the South Pole. Did you know it is the highest, driest, and windiest continent in the world?

Antarctica is also the coldest place on earth. The **interior** of

Antarctica is always covered with snow and ice. It took millions of years for this ice sheet to form. Strong winds sweep across the ice. The winds blow loose snow into blizzards. Very little snow actually falls. In the interior, near the South Pole, the temperature can drop to –94° F (-70°C) in winter. It's not quite as cold around the coastline. But, even in summer, coastal temperatures reach only -5°F (-15°C).

Antarctica is like a cold desert, making it a **harsh** place for people and animals to live. There is no life in the interior. In summer, a few **hardy** plants grow near the coast. The coastal areas are also alive with the cries of seabirds and the sounds of penguins and seals. Many kinds of whales live in the sea along with dolphins and porpoises. All these animals feed on the **abundant** fish in the sea.

No **permanent** human residents live on Antarctica. Scientists are allowed to live there for short periods of time. There are usually about 1000 scientists living in research stations. The only other visitors are tourists, who come to watch the wildlife. Garbage is a problem in Antarctica because there is no way to **dispose** of it. So, all garbage must be taken away by ship.

The year is divided into two seasons: summer and winter. In the summer, the sun never sets. There are 24 hours of daylight. The sea ice melts and huge icebergs break off the floating ice. Summer is the busy time, when scientists work and visitors come. For six months, during the harsh winter, there are 24 hours of darkness. The sea around Antarctica freezes solid.

> A *continent* is a large land mass. There are seven continents in the world: Africa, Antarctica, Asia, Australia, Europe, North America and South America. Every country in the world is situated in one of these continents. For example: Italy is situated in Europe, Canada is situated in North America, and India is situated in Asia.

Antarctica is an amazing *continent*. One hundred and fifty million years ago, it had a warm climate and green forests. Now this frozen land contains 90 percent of the world's ice.

Discussion

If you visited Antartica, what would you pack in your suitcase?

Check your understanding

 Circle the best meaning for each bold-faced word. Try to figure out what the word means by looking at the way it is used in the sentence.

1. The **interior** is the part of a country that is farthest away from the coast or the borders.
   a. the inside
   b. the outside
   c. around the edges

2. Greenland is often said to have a **harsh** climate because of its cold winter.
   a. agreeable
   b. pleasing
   c. unpleasant

3. Only **hardy** animals like the Arctic fox can live in very cold temperatures.
   a. able to hunt for food
   b. able to put up with cold and hardship
   c. able to move to warmer places

4. Tropical rain forests are **abundant** with wildlife because there is plenty of food and water.
   a. less than enough
   b. not many
   c. plentiful

5. A house is a **permanent** place to live, but a tent is not a **permanent** home.
   a. for a long time
   b. for a short time
   c. for a holiday

6. Some ships **dispose** of their garbage by dumping it into the sea.
   a. to keep
   b. to go in different directions
   c. to get rid of

Boost your understanding

 Circle the answer that makes the most sense.

1. The **interior** of a country will not have
   a. a train station.
   b. an airport.
   c. a seaport.

2. A **harsh** sound will
   a. hurt your ears.
   b. put you to sleep.
   c. please people who like listening to music.

3. If a company advertises a job for a **hardy** person, it wants
   a. a person who likes to work indoors.
   b. a person who can work outdoors in any weather.
   c. a person who hates cold weather.

4. If your garden has an **abundant** crop of carrots, you
   a. will be eating tomatoes instead of carrots.
   b. could be eating carrots for a long time.
   c. will be buying carrots at the supermarket.

5. A **permanent** resident of a city is someone who
   a. is visiting friends in the city.
   b. is living in the city on a full-time basis.
   c. has never lived in the city but would like to.

6. At the end of a day, a restaurant might **dispose** of
   a. customers.
   b. delicious meals.
   c. leftover food.

Expand your understanding

C Complete each sentence by writing the correct vocabulary word in the space.

Vocabulary words

| interior | hardy | permanent |
| harsh | abundant | dispose |

1. Jose made a living painting the _____ walls in buildings.

2. The grape juice made a _____ stain on the white tablecloth.

3. There was an _____ supply of text books, so no one had to share.

4. Forgetting about your problems is sometimes a good way to _____ of them.

5. The singer's voice became _____ from the smoke in the pub.

6. People who want to visit Antarctica are likely to be _____.

"freeze-up"

They have to get their boat out of the water before "freeze-up."

"Freeze up" is the time when the temperature drops below freezing. That's when the land, rivers, and lakes in the north freeze.

Apply your understanding

 Write sentences using the vocabulary words.

interior _____

_____

harsh _____

_____

hardy _____

_____

abundant _____

_____

permanent _____

_____

dispose _____

_____

Extend your understanding

In the passage, the word **interior** is used to describe the middle of the Antarctica. The outside of the continent would be described as the **exterior**. Exterior is the opposite of interior.

 Write the **opposite** of these words by dropping the prefix *in* and replacing it with *ex* or *out*.

1. inside _____

2. indoors _____

3. inhale _____

4. inward _____

5. input _____

Lesson 12

Popular Culture

The Slow Food Movement

Pre-reading Activity

What do you KNOW about the slow food movement?	What do you WANT to learn about the slow food movement?	What did you LEARN about the slow food movement?*

* Complete this column after you read the passage on the next page.

Photo: Sheri Bigelow

Vocabulary words

convenient	pace	specialties
hectic	counteract	produce

The Slow Food Movement

Fast food is **convenient** for people who lead **hectic** lives. Workers stop for a quick breakfast. People grab lunch on the run. Families pick up hamburgers or pizza for dinner. Fast food is a part of North American culture. Most people do not give it a second thought.

However, a food writer named Carlo Petrini got upset when a McDonald's restaurant opened next to a famous church in Rome. Petrini worried that fast food would make Italians change their eating habits. Italians took time to enjoy shopping for food, cooking, and socializing over a meal. Eating great food with family and friends was important to the Italian way of life. Petrini did not want this to change. He decided to do something to protect the Italian way of life.

Petrini started the slow food movement. This organization promotes a slower lifestyle. The movement wants people to take control of how they live. The fast **pace** of modern life can cause stress. Taking time to prepare and eat good food is a way to **counteract** stress. The slow food movement now has more than 80,000 members in 100 countries.

Slow food is the opposite of fast food. Fast food chains serve the same food in Los Angeles or Toronto. They make food taste the same no matter where you live. The point of slow food is to eat food from your local area. Petrini worried that local **specialties** and tastes might die out. In time, no one would make real beer, special hams and sausages, or local cheeses. Eating local specialties would be impossible. Instead, everyone would eat hamburgers and fries, fried chicken, and tacos.

The slow food movement encourages people to shop for local food. Farmer's markets are a good place to find fresh **produce** and local specialties. Petrini wants people to love good food. He suggests making your own pasta sauce using homegrown tomatoes or squeezing fresh oranges for juice. If Petrini has his way, slow food might become more popular than fast food.

————

Discussion

What are the local specialties of your area?

Check your understanding

 Circle the best meaning for each bold-faced word. Try to figure out what the word means by looking at the way it is used in the sentence.

1. A diaper service is a **convenient** way to clean diapers.
   a. difficult
   b. easy
   c. delicious

2. Habib's day was very **hectic** because he delivered 60 pizzas.
   a. busy and without rest
   b. boring and inactive
   c. hard-working

3. The **pace** of life in the country is slower than in the city.
   a. opening
   b. outlook
   c. speed

4. Many people add sugar to coffee to **counteract** the bitter taste.
   a. undo
   b. attack
   c. enjoy the results

5. It's a treat to eat the **specialties** of an area because they are always good.
   a. tasteless products
   b. ordinary products
   c. special products

6. Anyone can grow **produce** if they have a garden.
   a. tea and coffee
   b. fruits and vegetables
   c. cakes and cookies

Boost your understanding

 Circle the answer that makes the most sense.

1. A **convenient** store would be
   a. close to your house.
   b. on the other side of town.
   c. never open.

2. The best way to describe a **hectic** lifestyle is
   a. dull with very little happening.
   b. calm and restful.
   c. too many things to do and not enough time.

3. The baby grew at a fast **pace** and
   a. did not get taller.
   b. her clothes became too small.
   c. did not gain weight.

4. To **counteract** the effects of a full stomach, you could
   a. eat a heavy meal.
   b. drink pop.
   c. skip the next meal.

5. When a waiter tells you about the restaurant's **specialties**, he'll
   a. sing happy birthday.
   b. describe some dishes that the chef has made that day.
   c. try to persuade you to eat more.

6. If you went to a farmer's market to buy local **produce**, you might pick up
   a. ice cream.
   b. strawberries and cucumbers.
   c. crackers and popcorn.

Expand your understanding

C Complete each sentence by writing the correct vocabulary word in the space.

Vocabulary words

convenient	pace	specialties
hectic	counteract	produce

---

1. Maple sugar is one of the _____ you might eat in Quebec.

2. A runner with a good, even _____ is likely to win the race.

3. It's more _____ to take the bus into the city than to find a parking space.

4. Fresh _____ can go bad quickly in hot weather.

5. You can _____ the sting of sunburn by putting lotion on your skin.

6. The busy mother complained about the _____ day.

"Egg on your face."

Jake bought a used car. He boasted about his good deal, but when it broke down he had "egg on his face."

You get "egg on your face" when you've been outsmarted. Naturally, this makes you feel embarrassed.

Apply your understanding

 Write sentences using the vocabulary words.

pace _____

_____

convenient _____

_____

specialities _____

_____

hectic _____

_____

counteract _____

_____

produce _____

_____

Extend your understanding

The word **produce** has different meanings.
In this passage, the word **produce** means fruits and vegetables.
Here are some other meaning for the word **produce**:

1. To make or manufacture
   Example: This factory produces steel.

2. To create
   Example: She will produce a play.

3. To bring forth or yield
   Example: This tree produces lots of fruit.

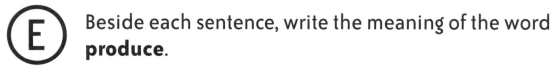 **(E)** Beside each sentence, write the meaning of the word **produce**.

1. There was lots of cheap **produce** in the corner store. _____

2. How many eggs can a chicken **produce** in a day? _____

3. The artist will **produce** a painting. _____

4. They hoped the bees would **produce** lots of honey. _____

5. These windmills **produce** energy. _____

6. The generator **produces** the electricity. _____

Crossword Puzzle 3

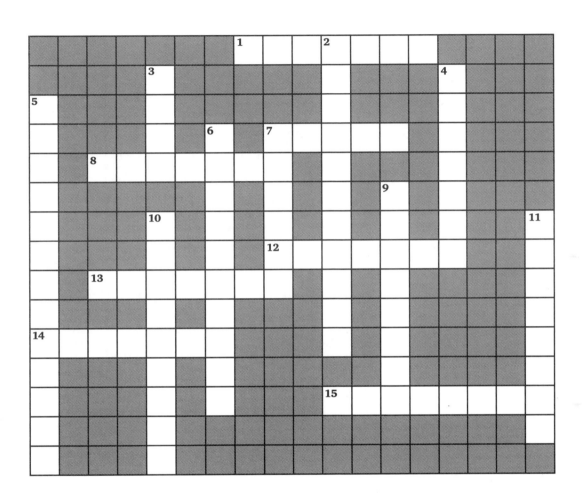

ACROSS

1. Fruits and vegtables
7. Able to put up with cold and hardship
8. To get rid of
12. To come without being invited or wanted
13. Lasting for a long time
14. A way through
15. The inside

DOWN

2. Not having enough
3. To droop or hang down
4. Move rapidly back and forth
5. A wrong idea
6. Easy to find
7. A synonym for busy
9. Plentiful
10. Able to do many things
11. Likes to be alone

Wordsearch 3

The letters in the word search puzzle form words. Circle the words listed below in the word search puzzle. The words are horizontal, vertical, diagonal, and backwards.

abundant	intrude
chronic	misconception
convenient	passage
deprivation	produce
dispose	sags
hardy	solitary
hectic	versatile
interior	vibrate

Lesson 13

Hair Loss

Pre-reading Activity

What do you KNOW about hair loss?	What do you WANT to learn about hair loss?	What did you LEARN about hair loss?*

* Complete this column after you read the passage on the next page.

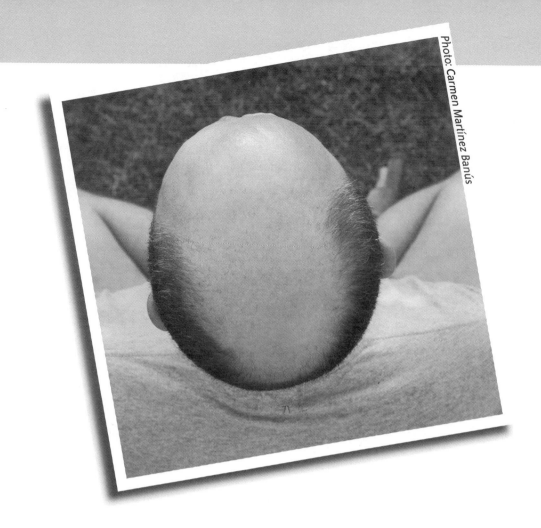

Photo: Carmen Martínez Banús

Hair Loss

Men and women can suffer from hair loss or baldness. It occurs much more often in men. Total baldness in women is **rare**. Baldness runs in families and is **hereditary**. This condition can be inherited from either parent.

> A hair *follicle* is a narrow opening on the surface of the skin. It contains cells that produce hair.

Each hair grows from a hair *follicle*. In bald men the male hormone, **testosterone**, causes the problem. Testosterone breaks down into a substance that shrinks hair follicles. The result is baldness, which occurs when hairs can no longer grow from follicles.

Bald men often have **bushy** beards or hairy chests. Their sensitivity to testosterone actually helps the growth of beards and chest hair. No one knows why this sensitivity produces opposite effects on different parts of the body.

Baldness is more likely to occur as men grow older. Around 40 percent of men have some hair loss by age 35. Hair loss follows a typical pattern. First, a **receding** hairline develops. Then, the hair on the top of the head begins to thin. In time, the two bald areas meet. The remaining thin, fine hair grows slowly.

Hair loss cannot be prevented. Often men try to hide or disguise bald spots. They wear wigs or comb hair over the bald spot. However, it is now more popular to leave the hair as it is, or to shave it off completely.

There are a few treatments to replace hair loss. These treatments do not work for everyone. Some medications can halt hair loss and promote hair growth. Surgery is the only **reliable** way to replace lost hair. Individual hairs are transplanted from areas where hair is still growing to the bald part of the head. The surgeon may take as many as 30 to 40 hairs or as few as 1 to 4 hairs. It takes several treatments to fill in the bald areas. These treatments cost a lot of money and they have no guarantee of success.

In the past, hair loss embarrassed people. However, attitudes to bald men have changed. Bald heads are now popular. In fact, many men who are not naturally bald now shave their heads!

Discussion

Why do you think some people try to disguise hair loss?

Check your understanding

 Circle the best meaning for each bold-faced word. Try to figure out what the word means by looking at the way it is used in the sentence.

1. It is **rare** to see snow in summer.
   a. common
   b. terrible
   c. uncommon

2. Blue eyes are **hereditary**. So, if you have blue eyes your child might also have blue eyes.
   a. passed down from parents to children
   b. something to do with hormones
   c. not able to be passed on

3. Some people think that men who have a high level of **testosterone** are aggressive.
   a. a test for men
   b. a female hormone
   c. a male hormone

4. A man with a **bushy** beard can look untidy because his beard is big.
   a. balding
   b. thick
   c. black

5. If you have a **receding** hairline your forehead will look big. This is because your hair is farther back on your head.
   a. going back
   b. coming forward
   c. disappearing

6. A **reliable** friend will never keep you waiting.
   a. unkind
   b. dependable
   c. old

Boost your understanding

 Circle the answer that makes the most sense.

1. It is **rare** to celebrate someone's 100th birthday because
    a. a person who is 100 doesn't like parties.
    b. it's hard to get that many candles on a cake.
    c. very few people live to be 100.

2. A **hereditary** trait is passed on from parents to children. Which of the following is <u>not</u> a hereditary trait?
    a. a person's eye colour
    b. a person's hair colour
    c. a person's favourite colour

3. **Testosterone** is a male hormone. It is responsible for many of the differences between men and women. Testosterone is responsible for
    a. the colour of men's skin.
    b. the facial hair on men.
    c. the colour of men's hair.

4. A person with a **bushy** hairstyle is likely to have
    a. straight, thin hair.
    b. bald spots.
    c. lots of thick hair.

5. In the spring, the snow in parks is **receding**. That means
    a. the park has piles of snow.
    b. the snow covers the grass.
    c. the snow in the park is slowly melting.

6. If a worker is **reliable**, it means that she
    a. is always on time and her work is good.
    b. makes careless mistakes.
    c. is often late.

Expand your understanding

 C Complete each sentence by writing the correct vocabulary word in the space.

Vocabulary words

rare	testosterone	receding
hereditary	bushy	reliable

---

1. People were happy to see the river water _____ after the flood.

2. Young men have more _____ than older men.

3. Most travelers don't like waiting, so they want a _____ train service.

4. His _____ moustache looked like a dead mouse under his nose.

5. It is _____ to see a school teacher with purple hair.

6. Red hair and freckles can be a _____ trait.

"hare-brained"

It was a "hare-brained" idea to shave my head in the winter.

When you say something is "hare-brained," you mean it is foolish, not sensible.

Apply your understanding

 Write sentences using the vocabulary words.

rare _____

_____

hereditary _____

_____

testosterone _____

_____

bushy _____

_____

receding _____

_____

reliable _____

_____

Extend your understanding

> A prefix is a part of the word that comes before the root word. A prefix has its own meaning.

You can add the prefix **un** to some words to get the opposite meaning.

A **reliable** friend is someone you can depend on.
An **unreliable** friend is someone you cannot depend on.

 How many pairs of words can you think of that use **un** for the opposite meaning? Here are some to get you started.

- cover and uncover
- fit and unfit
- like and unlike

_____   _____

_____   _____

_____   _____

You can check your answers in the dictionary.

Lesson 14

Zebra Mussels

Pre-reading Activity

What do you KNOW about zebra mussels?	What do you WANT to learn about zebra mussels?	What did you LEARN about zebra mussels?*

* Complete this column after you read the passage on the next page.

Photo: S. VanMechelen, University of Amsterdam

Vocabulary words

clusters	havoc	clog
filter	native	accumulate

Zebra Mussels

Mussels are common shellfish living in salt and fresh water. They have hard shells and soft bodies. If you live near the sea, you might see **clusters** of saltwater mussels attached to rocks. Freshwater mussels are harder to see. They dig into sand at the bottom of streams and lakes.

Watching mussels is *not* an exciting activity. They don't move. Their food comes to them. A mussel eats by opening its shell and pulling water inside. The water contains tiny plants and animals called plankton. Mussels **filter** water through their bodies, taking in oxygen and food.

Most mussels are useful. They purify water as they filter it through their bodies. They provide food for humans and other animals. We can tell how clean seas and lakes are by the health of mussels. When they die in great numbers, we know that water is polluted.

The zebra mussel, however, is a big pest. These animals are new arrivals to North America. They traveled here in ships from Europe. Since they arrived in 1989, these small mussels have created **havoc** in the Great Lakes.

Zebra mussels reproduce more quickly than do **native** mussels. A female can produce 30,000 to 100,000 eggs a year. Growing populations of zebra mussels eat huge amounts of plankton. Plankton is also the main source of food for young fish. Zebra mussels eat so much that there is no food left for the fish. They also attach themselves to native mussels' shells. The native mussels can't feed, and starve to death. Zebra mussels also **clog** the water intake pipes of drinking water facilities and industries. Every year, it costs hundreds of thousands of dollars to clear mussels from the intake pipes.

Zebra mussels may also be a health hazard to humans and animals. They **accumulate** pollution in their bodies. Eating the mussels is not a healthy choice. When the mussels spread onto swimming beaches, their sharp shells cut swimmers' feet.

While native mussels are good for lakes and streams, zebra mussels are definitely not.

Discussion
Can you think of some other small animals that are pests? Why do you consider them pests?

Check your understanding

 Circle the best meaning for each bold-faced word. Try to figure out what the word means by looking at the way it is used in the sentence.

1. The rock was covered with clams gathered together in **clusters.**
   a. squares
   b. odd numbers
   c. groups

2. The campers needed to **filter** the dirty water, so it would be safe to drink.
   a. drink
   b. wash
   c. purify

3. The **havoc** caused by the tornado was a disaster for the small town.
   a. destruction
   b. life
   c. bad smell

4. Kangaroos are **native** to Australia.
   a. come from another country
   b. born in the country they live in
   c. from another time

5. An accident on the highway can **clog** the roads and cause a traffic jam.
   a. block
   b. decay
   c. smell

6. Basil liked to **accumulate** books so he opened a second-hand bookstore.
   a. count
   b. collect or gather
   c. pass out

Boost your understanding

 Circle the answer that makes the most sense.

1. You could buy **clusters** of bananas. What else could you buy in **clusters?**
   a. watermelons
   b. grapes
   c. apples

2. Buildings **filter** the air to make it clean. To run properly, a car must **filter**
   a. the sound.
   b. the oil, air, and gas.
   c. the coffee.

3. A tornado can create **havoc**. Something else that creates **havoc** is
   a. a hurricane.
   b. a library.
   c. a full moon.

4. Arlo was born in the United States, but he now lives in Canada. Arlo is a **native** of
   a. Mexico
   b. Canada
   c. United States

5. Tea leaves can **clog** a drain. Another thing that could clog drains would be
   a. apple juice.
   b. hot chocolate.
   c. coffee grounds.

6. If you had a very small apartment, you would not want to **accumulate**
   a. junk.
   b. money.
   c. friends.

Expand your understanding

 Complete each sentence by writing the correct vocabulary word in the space.

Vocabulary words

clusters	havoc	clog
filter	native	accumulate

---

1. If the roof has a hole in it, rain may _____ through it.

2. Wilma is a _____ of Canada and she speaks French and English.

3. If you _____ a toilet, you have to unblock it before someone uses it.

4. When I _____ enough money, I will buy a mountain bike.

5. The snowstorm created _____ at the airport.

6. In the spring, you will see _____ of tulips.

"clam up"

idiom for today

"Why do you always "clam up" when I ask about your partner?" Fay asked her friend, Kara. "I'm beginning to think she doesn't exist."

If you "clam up," you suddenly stop talking and become quiet.

Apply your understanding

 Write sentences using the vocabulary words.

clusters _____

_____

filter _____

_____

havoc _____

_____

native _____

_____

clog _____

_____

accumulate _____

_____

Extend your understanding

Everyone is a **native** of someplace. You might be a native of the United States, Canada, Vietnam, or some other country. Your **native** land is the country where you were born. We can use other words to describe our **native** land, such as birthplace, home, homeland, motherland, and fatherland.

We also use the word **native** as a name for the original people of a country. The term Native Americans refers to the Aboriginal people of America. Other terms for Aboriginal people are Indigenous and First Nations.

The word **native** is also used to describe plants or animals that come from a certain place. For example, koala bears are native to Australia, but rabbits are not native to Australia. That means koala bears are from Australia, but rabbits were brought into Australia from Europe.

 Test your knowledge of **native** things. You may want to work with a partner or in groups. You can search the Internet or the library for answers.

1. Which of the following is *not* the name of a native North American tribe?
   a. Cree
   b. Sioux
   c. Maori

2. The name given to wild cats that are native to North America is
   a. cougars
   b. tigers
   c. lions

3. Chocolate is made from the bean of the cacao tree. This tree is native to
   a. Australia
   b. Central and South America
   c. North America

Lesson 15

Wind Power

Pre-reading Activity

What do you KNOW about wind power?	What do you WANT to learn about wind power?	What did you LEARN about wind power?*

* Complete this column after you read the passage on the next page.

Photo: Scott Cressman

Vocabulary words

obsolete	renewable	graze
depleted	rotate	potential

Wind Power

Have you ever tried to walk against a strong wind? If so, you know how powerful wind can be.

Wind is a good source of energy because it is so powerful. In the past, farmers used windmills to grind flour and to pump water for crops and animals. These windmills produced energy on a small scale. Then, coal, oil, and natural gas were developed to provide energy on a large scale. Windmills became **obsolete**.

Our use of coal, oil, and natural gas has steadily increased. This is a problem because there is a limited amount of these resources. Once these resources are **depleted**, they will be gone forever. Some people fear that we might run out of coal, oil, and gas. That is why **renewable** sources of energy, such as wind power, are once again becoming important. Wind power is now used to make electricity on a larger scale.

Modern windmills are called turbines. They have three huge blades that face into the wind. The wind forces the blades to **rotate** at 10 to 30 revolutions per minute. This force spins a rod inside the turbine. The rod is connected to a generator, which produces the electricity.

Wind farms are places that contain hundreds of turbines. There are many benefits to wind farms. First, they produce electricity in a way that does not hurt the environment. Second, the grass growing underneath the turbines can be used to **graze** animals. Finally, if the turbines are taken down, the land remains undamaged.

There are, however, some disadvantages to wind farms. Electricity produced from wind is more expensive than other sources of electricity. It can cost billions of dollars to transport electricity from wind farms to cities. As well, many people do not want to live near the ever-present noise from the turbines. Other people think that wind farms spoil natural landscapes.

Despite these problems, wind power has **potential**. By using renewable sources of energy, we are helping the earth rather than damaging it.

Discussion

What changes would we need to make to our lifestyle if we ran out of coal, oil, and gas?

Check your understanding

 Circle the best meaning for each bold-faced word. Try to figure out what the word means by looking at the way it is used in the sentence.

1. The garage sale had **obsolete** items, like a turntable for playing records.
   a. nice to look at
   b. no longer in use
   c. run-down

2. A long, hot, and dry summer **depleted** the city's water resources.
   a. used up
   b. made up
   c. planned

3. The oceans provide **renewable** resources, such as fish.
   a. always new
   b. can be replaced
   c. gone forever

4. The wheels on a bicycle **rotate.**
   a. run over
   b. go backwards
   c. turn around

5. Cows **graze** in fields when they are hungry.
   a. grow
   b. cut down
   c. feed on grass

6. It often does not snow in the winter, but there is always the **potential** for a snowstorm.
   a. possibility at some time in the future
   b. no possibility
   c. certainly

Boost your understanding

 Circle the answer that makes the most sense.

1. **Obsolete** things in our homes generally end up
   a. in the kitchen.
   b. in the garbage.
   c. in the bedroom.

2. Gil **depleted** his bank account by eating out. This means
   a. Gil didn't have any money in his account.
   b. Gil spent only a small amount on eating out.
   c. Gil was saving up to eat at his favourite restaurant.

3. Solar energy is a **renewable** resource. This means
   a. in time we will run out of energy from the sun.
   b. there is an endless supply of energy from the sun.
   c. energy from the sun is expensive.

4. Some office chairs **rotate**. You can make them
   a. go up and down.
   b. spin around.
   c. move across the floor.

5. Examples of animals that **graze** on grass are
   a. butterflies, ants, beetles, and bees.
   b. ducks, swans, pigeons, and eagles.
   c. deer, cattle, sheep, and horses.

6. If a child shows great **potential** in math, it's likely that she
   a. will fail math.
   b. will study math in college.
   c. will not like math.

Expand your understanding

 Complete each sentence by writing the correct vocabulary word in the space.

Vocabulary words

obsolete	renewable	graze
depleted	rotate	potential

---

1. Looking after six children _____ our father's energy.

2. Kim asked the mechanic if he would _____ the wheels on her car.

3. When I'm by myself, I like to _____ on food all night.

4. Drivers' licences are _____ for a fee.

5. If a mother loves music, there is a _____ that her child will too.

6. Our fridge is _____, so we can't get parts to repair it.

"windbag"

Nestor is bragging about winning the game again.
He is a "windbag."

A person who talks too much is a "windbag."

Apply your understanding

 Write sentences using the vocabulary words.

obsolete _____

_____

depleted _____

_____

renewable _____

_____

rotate _____

_____

graze _____

_____

potential _____

_____

Extend your understanding

> A prefix is a part of the word that comes before the root word. A prefix has its own meaning.

You have learned the meaning of **renewable**. **Nonrenewable** has the opposite meaning.

The prefix *non* means **not**. When you put *non* at the beginning of a word, it gives the root word the opposite meaning.

Here's an example: smoker—non-smoker. A non-smoker is someone who does not smoke.

 Write the opposites of these words and their meanings.

Word	Opposite	Meaning
profit	_____	_____
fiction	_____	_____
toxic	_____	_____
stop	_____	_____
dairy	_____	_____

Use your dictionary to check the meanings.

Lesson 16

Tattoos

Pre-reading Activity

What do you KNOW about the tattoos?	What do you WANT to learn about tattoos?	What did you LEARN about tattoos?*

* Complete this column after you read the passage on the next page.

Photo: Karina Tischlinger

Vocabulary words

offence	represented	trend
committed	rank	fashionable

Tattoos

Tattoos are an old form of body art in many cultures. In the past, people got tattoos for many reasons. In ancient Rome, tattoos were used to mark slaves. In ancient China, a famous story describes a general who had a tattoo drawn on his back. The tattoo reminded him to be loyal to his country. In Borneo, warriors who had killed in battle had tattoos drawn on their hands. These marks brought them respect.

In Japan, a criminal's first **offence** was marked with a tattooed line across his forehead. Another curved line marked a second offence. If the criminal **committed** a third offence, he received a third line. These three lines made up the Japanese word for "dog." Many years later, tattoos became highly regarded in Japan. Royalty were the only people who were allowed to wear fancy clothes. So, people began to decorate their bodies with tattoos.

In South Pacific cultures, tattooing was also very important. The word "tattoo" comes from this area. It means "to puncture the skin." The people thought that tattoos **represented** a person's energy. All through their lives, people added tattoos to their bodies. In New Zealand, the Maoris tattooed their faces to show their **rank** in the family.

Tattoos were not common in Europe until the late 1700s. Captain Cook brought a tattooed man back from the South Pacific. The sight of this man's tattoos started a fashion **trend**. This trend did not last a long time.

Tattoos became unpopular when sailors and gang members started getting them. Also, heavily tattooed men and women found work in circuses. Tattooed people were not respected. Tattoos began to shock people.

This negative attitude towards tattoos has changed. Film stars and musicians began to get tattoos. This made tattoos **fashionable** again. Now, tattoos are popular with all ages. Even a Barbie doll has a butterfly tattoo. Now that tattoos are common again, it is likely that their popularity will fall. After all, tattoos are more often out of fashion than in fashion.

Discussion

Why do you think some people get laser surgery to remove their tattoos?

Check your understanding

 Circle the best meaning for each bold-faced word. Try to figure out what the word means by looking at the way it is used in the sentence.

1. Stealing, murder, and rape are each an **offence** in our society.
   a. escape
   b. illegal act
   c. capture

2. Joe **committed** a crime. Later, he turned himself into the police.
   a. did
   b. saw
   c. heard

3. The beaver was carved into the totem pole. The beavers **represented** the land.
   a. were a picture of
   b. were a carving of
   c. were a symbol of

4. A general has the highest **rank** in the army.
   a. name of a person
   b. position
   c. pay

5. Young people are more likely to follow a **trend** than senior citizens.
   a. current style
   b. something that is out of style
   c. mistake

6. People often copy movie stars because they wear **fashionable** clothes.
   a. clothes or objects that look strange
   b. clothes or objects from the past
   c. clothes or objects that are popular

Boost your understanding

 Circle the answer that makes the most sense.

1. It is an **offence** to
   a. walk your dog.
   b. steal money.
   c. plant flowers.

2. If someone **committed** a crime, she
   a. tried to catch a thief.
   b. did something illegal.
   c. ate too much food.

3. At the Olympic games, the flags **represented**
   a. all the countries that took part in the games.
   b. a beautiful display of colours.
   c. something for the athletes to carry.

4. At Dan's workplace, holiday times are fixed according to **rank**, so
   a. people in a higher position or rank get first choice.
   b. people with no ranking get first choice.
   c. everybody gets the same holiday times.

5. Fashion **trends** are likely to
   a. tell you what is cheap.
   b. tell you what is new and popular.
   c. tell you what is old and unpopular.

6. If Rosa wants to be **fashionable**, she will wear
   a. her grandmother's clothes.
   b. the same type of clothes every year.
   c. new styles of clothes.

Expand your understanding

C Complete each sentence by writing the correct vocabulary word in the space.

Vocabulary words

offence	represented	trend
committed	rank	fashionable

---

1. The teenager _____ a crime by throwing a brick through a shop window.

2. He gave her roses, because they _____ love.

3. Skateboarding is still a popular _____ among teenagers.

4. The reporter asked Leo his _____ in the army.

5. This year, everyone thinks it's _____ to wear baggy clothes.

6. Armed robbery is an _____ that will put a criminal behind bars.

"Keep up with the times."

idiom for today

Sam "keeps up with the times" by watching the music shows on television.

"Keeping up with the times" means being aware of the latest trends.

Apply your understanding

 Write sentences using the vocabulary words.

offence _____

_____

committed _____

_____

represented _____

_____

rank _____

_____

trend _____

_____

fashionable _____

_____

Extend your understanding

The word **fashion** came into use over 500 years ago. Since then, fashions have changed many times. Things that were **fashionable** when you were young are now **old-fashioned**.

The words **fashion** and **trends** are often used together. Someone who sets **fashion trends** is called a trendsetter. Sometimes, we say a fashionable person looks **hot**. The only thing that is constant about **fashion** is that it changes.

(E) In your opinion, what are some fashion trends?

_____   _____

_____   _____

_____   _____

What was fashionable when you were a teenager?

Example: straight hair, short skirts, The Beatles

_____   _____

_____   _____

_____   _____

Crossword Puzzle 4

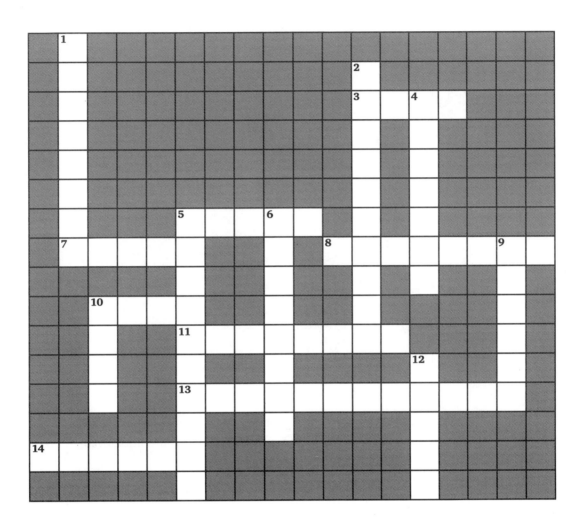

ACROSS

3. To block a drain
5. Widespread destruction
7. Feed on growing grass
8. Groups of similar things
10. Uncommon
11. Used up
13. Male hormone
14. To purify

DOWN

1. Going back
2. To collect or gather
4. An illegal act
5. Passed down from parent to child
6. No longer in use
9. To spin around
10. Position in a group
12. Current style

Wordsearch 4

The letters in the word search puzzle form words. Circle the words listed below in the word search puzzle. The words are horizontal, vertical, diagonal, and backwards.

accumulate	obsolete
clog	offense
clusters	rank
depleted	rare
filter	receding
graze	rotate
havoc	testosterone
hereditary	trend

Donating Blood

Pre-reading Activity

What do you KNOW about donating blood?	What do you WANT to learn about donating blood?	What did you LEARN about donating blood?*

* Complete this column after you read the passage on the next page.

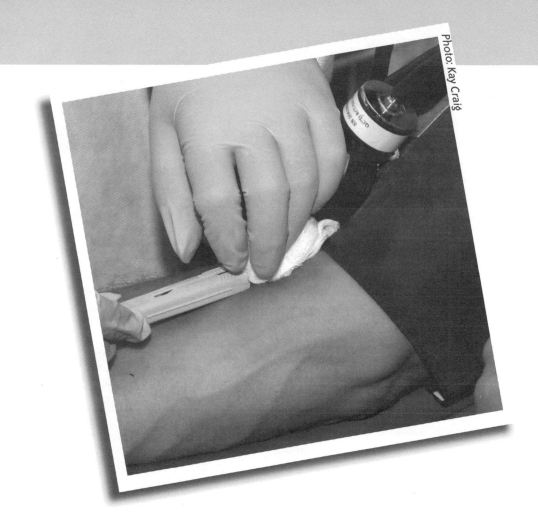

Photo: Kay Craig

Vocabulary words

ensures	anemic	initially
acquired	discarded	strenuous

Donating Blood

Donated blood is an essential part of our health care system. Hospitals rely on blood donations to perform operations and treat accident victims. Blood is used to treat diseases such as cancer. New medical technologies, such as joint replacements and organ transplants, increase the demand for blood.

Almost any healthy adult can donate blood. However, each donor must have a confidential screening test before each session. The donated blood is examined to see if it contains viruses or diseases, such as HIV, malaria, or the common cold. The test **ensures** that the patient who receives the blood will not be infected with a disease. It takes very little time to donate blood. You must eat before donating, so that you will not faint during the session. Before you donate blood, the nurse will test your iron level. A drop of blood is **acquired** by pricking your finger. Your blood is tested to see if you are **anemic**. If your red blood cell count is good, you can donate blood.

The blood donation procedure is safe. It takes between 10 to 15 minutes. A nurse inserts a needle into your vein. You will feel a small prick, but the rest of the procedure is painless. All needles are sterile and **discarded** after each use. One unit of blood is collected. Adults have between eight to ten units of blood in their bodies. **Initially**, you may feel weak, but your body will quickly recover from this loss of blood. After giving blood, you relax for about ten minutes. You are advised not to do any **strenuous** activity for six hours.

You can donate blood several times a year. There are blood donor clinics in most cities. Mobile blood clinics often visit high schools, colleges, churches, and community centres.

Only 5 percent of the population donates blood. Yet, the need for blood increases by 9 percent each year. Donating blood is rewarding. It's possible that your blood donation will help save a life.

Discussion

Do you think there are any risks in donating or receiving blood?
If so, what are they?

Check your understanding

 Circle the best meaning for each bold-faced word. Try to figure out what the word means by looking at the way it is used in the sentence.

1. The nurse **ensures** that her patients are comfortable by checking them every few hours.
   a. stops something
   b. gives to someone
   c. makes certain

2. Our family wanted a dog, so we **acquired** one from the animal shelter.
   a. gave
   b. obtained or got
   c. took back

3. If you are **anemic,** you have less than the normal number of red blood cells.
   a. a condition that makes you tired
   b. a disease that makes you itchy
   c. a condition that causes you to have lots of energy

4. After opening her present, Ivy **discarded** the wrapping paper and put it in the garbage.
   a. put back
   b. got rid of
   c. kept safe

5. **Initially,** Paul wanted to be a welder, but later, he changed his mind.
   a. at the end
   b. in the middle
   c. at the beginning

6. Moving is a **strenuous** activity because you have to pack and lift many boxes.
   a. needing lots of effort
   b. gentle exercise
   c. lazy attitude

Boost your understanding

 Circle the answer that makes the most sense.

1. Ivan **ensures** that he has enough money for his rent by
   a. saving some of his money.
   b. spending all his money.
   c. not paying attention to how he spends money.

2. If you have **acquired** a tan, you probably have been
   a. sitting inside.
   b. sitting out in the sun.
   c. driving around.

3. If you are **anemic**, the doctor will probably suggest that you
   a. exercise more.
   b. eat less liver.
   c. take iron to build up your red blood cells.

4. If an old pair of boots is **discarded**, the boots are
   a. repaired.
   b. thrown out.
   c. used to plant flowers.

5. **Initially**, I felt angry when my dog died.
   a. after
   b. later
   c. at first

6. Running uphill is a **strenuous** activity. When you stop you are likely to be
   a. full of energy.
   b. out of breath.
   c. breathing normally.

Expand your understanding

 Complete each sentence by writing the correct vocabulary word in the space.

> **Vocabulary words**
>
> ensure   anemic   initially
>
> acquired   discarded   strenuous

1. Guy _____ many books from the second-hand bookstore.

2. Eating liver can help stop you from becoming _____ because it is rich in iron.

3. In order to _____ that we caught the last bus, we left the party early.

4. Picking fruit is a _____ job which does not pay well.

5. Annie _____ the worn out rug and bought a brand new one.

6. The baby _____ had blond hair, but as he got older his hair became brown.

"*Get blood from a stone.*" idiom for today

Asking Tina to pay back money is like trying to "get blood from a stone."

When you say a task is like trying to "get blood from a stone," you are saying it is very difficult to do.

Apply your understanding

 Write sentences using the vocabulary words.

ensure _____

_____

acquired _____

_____

anemic _____

_____

discarded _____

_____

initially _____

_____

strenuous _____

_____

Extend your understanding

Ensure and **insure** are often confused.

You cannot use one in place of the other. Let's take a look at the meaning of each word.

- **Ensure** means to make certain.
  I want to **ensure** that you know when the movie starts.

- **Insure** means to make an agreement to pay money to a company.
  The company agrees to pay you if something happens (e.g., you get sick,
  your house burns down, your car is damaged). This is called insurance.
  I want to **insure** my car for five thousand dollars.

 Now write a sentence using each word.

ensure _____

_____

insure _____

_____

Lesson 18

Wildlife

Killer Bees

Pre-reading Activity

What do you KNOW about killer bees?	What do you WANT to learn about killer bees?	What did you LEARN about killer bees?*

* Complete this column after you read the passage on the next page.

Photo: Jim Orr

Vocabulary words

experiment	offspring	adapt
breed	aggressive	ironically

Killer Bees

———

Killer bees are a result of an **experiment** that went wrong. In the 1950s, scientists in Brazil wanted to **breed** African bees with local honeybees. They hoped the **offspring** would produce more honey than the local honeybees did. They also hoped the offspring would be better suited to the jungle than the local honeybees were.

The scientists brought bees from Africa. They carefully bred the bees at their research station. One day, 26 African queen bees escaped from their hives.

The African bees began to breed with the local honeybees. Their offspring were nicknamed "killer bees." These bees bred faster than the local bees did and took over the area. The local honeybees died out because they could not compete with the killer bees.

> *Swarm* means a cluster of bees, led by a queen, that leave the hive to start a new colony. *Swarm* also means a large number of insects or birds moving together or in clusters.

Killer bees are **aggressive**. A noise or vibration can provoke them and they can stay angry for days. A person just walking near a hive can provoke killer bees. They will attack in large numbers. A *swarm* of killer bees may chase people or animals for up to a mile. When the bees attack, their victims can receive thousands of stings. A person can survive up to 300 stings. One killer bee attack in Costa Rica killed a young man. He received more than 10,000 stings.

Killer bees multiply quickly because of the way they breed and swarm. They are not fussy about where they build their nests. They will use hollow trees, walls, sheds, garbage containers, and old cars. Killer bees often leave their hives in swarms to set up new colonies. This increases the number of bees in an area.

Killer bees entered the United States in 1990. Since then, they have spread across the southern United States. Some scientists believe that killer bees will **adapt** to colder weather and spread even further north. **Ironically**, killer bees make five times less honey than other bees do. In time, the killer bees could destroy America's honey industry.

Discussion
How do you think the problem of killer bees can be solved?

Check your understanding

 Circle the best meaning for each bold-faced word. Try to figure out what the word means by looking at the way it is used in the sentence.

1. The Arctic would be a good place to do an **experiment** on cold weather and its effect on humans.
   a. a test to find out about something.
   b. a trip to experience cold weather.
   c. something that shows the way someone is feeling.

2. When a bull and a cow **breed**, the result is a calf.
   a. care for
   b. mate and produce offspring
   c. chase

3. The **offspring** of dogs are called puppies.
   a. young ones
   b. parents
   c. owners

4. Bee keepers find **aggressive** bees harder to raise because they sting quicker.
   a. likely to attack
   b. able to learn new tricks
   c. likely to buzz

5. A mother must **adapt** her sleep to fit her baby's schedule.
   a. have a good outlook
   b. adjust to the new situation
   c. look at a situation clearly

6. My friend is a traffic cop. **Ironically**, he just got fined for unpaid speeding tickets.
   a. the same as always
   b. positive about it
   c. opposite of what is expected

Boost your understanding

 Circle the answer that makes the most sense.

1. An example of an **experiment** might be
   a. riding a motorbike across the United States.
   b. testing three different cups to see which one keeps coffee the hottest.
   c. baking a cake by following a recipe from a book.

2. Many pet owners don't let their cat **breed** because
   a. breeding is not good for cats.
   b. they will have to find homes for the kittens.
   c. the cat won't be able to find its way home afterwards.

3. If a cat does breed, she will likely have **offspring**. A cat's offspring are called
   a. brothers and sisters.
   b. kittens.
   c. puppies.

4. An **aggressive** dog is likely to
   a. fight with other dogs.
   b. lick other dogs.
   c. stay away from other dogs.

5. Some older pets are adopted from shelters. But they can **adapt** to new homes. This means that
   a. they need special treatment.
   b. they will never be able to move again.
   c. they are able to live in different homes.

6. A friend gives you a birthday present. It's a cake. **Ironically**,
   a. you don't even like cake!
   b. you love cake!
   c. your friend loves baking.

Expand your understanding

C Complete each sentence by writing the correct vocabulary word in the space.

Vocabulary words

experiment	offspring	adapt
breed	aggressive	ironically

---

1. A grizzly bear will attack when humans go near her _____.

2. They waited over an hour for the bus. Then, _____, two buses came at the same time.

3. Farmers _____ their cattle in the spring.

4. Dee's orange hair was an _____ gone wrong.

5. Leroy could _____ to meeting people in new situations.

6. A grizzly bear can be _____ if humans go near her cubs.

"bee's knees"

"Kara thinks she is the 'bee's knees' in her new outfit," said her mother.

If you think you are the "bee's knees," you think you are better than anyone else. To be described as "the bee's knees" is to be the best.

Apply your understanding

 Write sentences using the vocabulary words.

experiment _____

_____

breed _____

_____

offspring _____

_____

aggressive _____

_____

adapt _____

_____

ironically _____

_____

Extend your understanding

The word **bee** is singular. If you add *s* to **bee**, it becomes plural, or more than one —
bees.

However, a few words are spelt the same whether they are singular or plural. For
example, **offspring** can be singular or plural. By looking at how the word is used
in the sentence, you will know if the writer is talking about one **offspring** or many
offspring.

 Look at these examples of animal words that can be
singular or plural. Write **P** if the bolded word is plural and
S if it is singular.

1. ___ We bought a **salmon** for our dinner.

2. ___ Wool comes from **sheep**.

3. ___ Carol caught a **fish** in the river.

4. ___ A painting of a **deer** won first prize.

5. ___ **Salmon** swim in the sea.

6. ___ Solomon bought a **trout** for his supper.

7. ___ **Deer** got into the garden and ate all the flowers.

8. ___ A **sheep** escaped from the field.

9. ___ Carol and Jim went fishing for **trout**.

10. ___ Small **fish** swam around our legs.

Can you think of some other animal words that can be both singular and plural?

_____   _____   _____   _____

Lesson 19

Environment

The Mountain that Walks

Pre-reading Activity

What do you KNOW about landslides?	What do you WANT to learn about landslides?	What did you LEARN about landslides?*

* Complete this column after you read the passage on the next page.

Photo: Steve Corbett

Vocabulary words

inhabitants	deposits	massive
loomed	tremors	devastation

The Mountain that Walks

One of the worst landslides in North America took place in 1903, in Frank, Alberta. Frank was a small mining town in western Canada. The 600 **inhabitants** lived in a steep-sided valley in the Crowsnest Pass. Turtle Mountain **loomed** over the town site. The native people of the area traditionally called Turtle Mountain "The Mountain That Walks."

Underneath this mountain were large **deposits** of coal. Coal mining began in 1901. By 1903, miners had dug deep into the mountain. Ground **tremors** shook the mine on a daily basis. They were an early warning of disaster. However, the miners got used to the tremors and even welcomed them. That's because the tremors loosened the coal, making the miners' work easier.

In the early morning hours of April 29, the residents of Frank were sleeping peacefully. Only the miners on the night shift were awake and active. Without warning, the summit of Turtle Mountain collapsed. The collapse triggered a huge avalanche of rock and snow. A **massive** chunk of limestone crashed down the mountain and buried part of the town. The rock fall was over 492 feet (150 m) deep. In less than two minutes, this slide spread over 1.2 square miles (3 square km) of the valley.

The mountain was unstable due to the soft limestone rock at the top. Bad weather conditions and the underground mining tunnels probably triggered the slide.

> *Rubble* is a loose mass of rocks broken by natural forces or by people. For example, the rocks that fell from the mountain are rubble. People make rubble when they pull down old buildings. The broken pieces of concrete are called rubble.

One hundred people lived in the path of the slide. Rock and mud crushed their houses in seconds. Seventy people were buried in their sleep. Rescuers recovered only 12 bodies. *Rubble* buried the mine entrance. Seventeen miners on the night shift were trapped underground. After 14 hours of digging, they freed themselves.

The mine reopened for a few years before shutting down again in 1911. The town's citizens gradually moved farther up the valley. Over 100 years later, you can see the debris from the slide. Turtle Mountain still looms over the **devastation**. It remains an unstable mountain. One day, it might again become "The Mountain That Walks."

Discussion

Does this tragedy remind you of any recent events? Which one(s)?

Check your understanding

 Circle the best meaning for each bold-faced word. Try to figure out what the word means by looking at the way it is used in the sentence.

1. The **inhabitants** of the town went to a meeting to plan a new park.
   a. people who are visiting an area
   b. people who live in an area
   c. tourists

2. The giraffe **loomed** over the small zoo keeper.
   a. appeared small and friendly
   b. appeared cold and wet
   c. appeared large and above

3. Men rushed to Alaska when **deposits** of gold were discovered there.
   a. manmade objects such as gold rings
   b. natural layers of sand, rock, or minerals
   c. equipment used to dig into the ground

4. An earthquake causes **tremors** in the ground and makes buildings vibrate.
   a. shaking movements
   b. stillness
   c. explosions

5. A **massive** rock fall will destroy everything in its path.
   a. tiny and light
   b. large and heavy
   c. black and white

6. The tidal wave caused **devastation** in the coastal areas.
   a. an area where trees have been cut down
   b. a dangerous mountain
   c. destruction

Boost your understanding

 B Circle the answer that makes the most sense.

1. In the inner city, most **inhabitants** live in
    a. apartments.
    b. farms.
    c. house boats.

2. Which of these animals would **loom** over a human?
    a. elephant
    b. mouse
    c. goat

3. Which of these is not made from **deposits** in the ground?
    a. a silver necklace
    b. a gold ring
    c. a leather watchstrap

4. A person might get **tremors** before he
    a. sang in public for the first time.
    b. ate a special meal.
    c. relaxed on the beach.

5. Most gardeners would rather not have a **massive** amount of
    a. roses.
    b. weeds.
    c. sweet peas.

6. The **devastation** caused by a fire would make a house look
    a. like a nice place to live.
    b. as if it needed a few repairs.
    c. like a ruin.

Expand your understanding

 Complete each sentence by writing the correct vocabulary word in the space.

> **Vocabulary words**
>
> inhabitants   deposits   massive
>
> loomed   tremors   devastation

1. A black cloud _____ over the children's picnic.

2. The _____ of the town were proud of their basketball team.

3. The bodybuilder had _____ muscles.

4. When Spike laughed, his deep voice sent _____ through the house.

5. Cash and cheques paid into a bank are called _____.

6. A hurricane caused _____ throughout Florida.

"off the beaten track" — idiom for today

"I like to explore places that are 'off the beaten track,' like Frank, Alberta."

If a place is "off the beaten track," it is away from the main road and often in a wilderness area.

Apply your understanding

 Write sentences using the vocabulary words.

inhabitants _____

_____

loomed _____

_____

deposits _____

_____

tremors _____

_____

massive _____

_____

devastation _____

_____

Extend your understanding

A synonym is a word that has the same, or nearly the same meaning, as another word.

These verbs are synonyms for the phrase **to live in:**
- inhabit
- occupy
- dwell
- reside

I **occupy** a third floor apartment.

These nouns are synonyms for **where people live:**
- dwelling
- residence
- apartment
- house
- home
- condo

My **home** is in another country.

These nouns are synonyms for **people who live somewhere:**
- inhabitants
- dwellers
- residents
- occupiers
- population
- homeowners

I am a **resident** of Mexico.

(E) Write three sentences using your choice of words to describe where you live.

_____

_____

_____

_____

Lesson 20

Superstitions

Pre-reading Activity

What do you KNOW about superstitions?	What do you WANT to learn about superstitions?	What did you LEARN about superstitions?*

* Complete this column after you read the passage on the next page.

Photo: Juan Olvido

Vocabulary words

rituals	token	taboo
avoid	psychological	tempt

Superstitions

—

Superstitions may seem silly. However, many people

perform **rituals** to prevent bad luck. For instance, some people
won't walk under ladders. Others **avoid** black cats. They believe it's
unlucky for a black cat to cross their path. Many people believe it's

bad luck to open an umbrella indoors. Some people believe certain dates are unlucky. When the 13th falls on Friday, people often take extra care.

On the other hand, many people perform **rituals** to encourage good luck. They might wear a lucky tie or a scarf to a job interview. Other people touch a piece of wood when they make a remark that they want to remain true. For instance, they say, "I've never had a car accident, touch wood." Some students put a lucky **token** in their pocket before a test. They believe this gives them a **psychological** advantage.

We are often most superstitious before performing important tasks. Rodeo cowboys believe that shaving before a competition will help them ride well. They also think that eating a hot dog will bring them luck. However, they believe that wearing yellow clothes or putting a hat on a bed brings bad luck. Cowboys aren't the only superstitious performers. Hockey star Wayne Gretzky tucked in the right side of his jersey for luck before every game.

Actors have their own set of **taboos**. They believe it's bad luck to whistle in the dressing room. Strangely enough, it's considered bad luck to wish an actor good luck! Instead, you should say, "break a leg." This could be because actors do not want to **tempt** fate by being too confident.

In North America, there are many common superstitutions. Perhaps you are familiar with some of them. Do you believe if you make a wish on a falling star, it will come true? Or breaking a mirror means seven years of bad luck? If you accidentally wear something inside out, do you expect a pleasant surprise? Will you always be in debt if you shave your head on a Saturday? Does an itchy palm means money is coming your way?

Don't worry if you are superstitious. Most superstitions are harmless, or even helpful.

Discussion

Do you perform any rituals to encourage good luck or prevent bad luck? If so, what are they?

Check your understanding

(A) Circle the best meaning for each bold-faced word. Try to figure out what the word means by looking at the way it is used in the sentence.

1. **Rituals**, such as reading to children before bedtime, have a positive effect on family life.
   a. things that are repeated regularly
   b. things that never get done
   c. things to ignore

2. You can **avoid** getting stung if you stay away from bees.
   a. leave something
   b. meet someone
   c. keep away from

3. Bruno gave the nurse a Bible as a **token** of his gratitude.
   a. a keepsake
   b. something to carry stuff in
   c. a prayer or a wish

4. Some **psychological** problems such as anxiety can be helped by thinking positively.
   a. in your stomach
   b. in your eyes
   c. in your mind

5. Picking flowers in city parks is **taboo** because it spoils the display for others.
   a. feared
   b. forbidden
   c. dramatic

6. Marie tried to **tempt** us to go skinny-dipping by telling us the water was warm.
   a. give in
   b. persuade
   c. hide from

Boost your understanding

 Circle the answer that makes the most sense.

1. Religious ceremonies usually include **rituals**. A religious **ritual** could be
   a. saying prayers.
   b. getting married.
   c. raising money for charity.

2. You may want to **avoid** your boss because
   a. you know a good joke that he would like.
   b. you want her to sign a letter.
   c. you don't want to be given any more work.

3. Sometimes we keep things as a **token** to remind us of events. In this case a token could be
   a. a ticket to a pop concert.
   b. a pet.
   c. a diary.

4. A psychiatrist helps people with **psychological** problems. A psychiatrist studies
   a. feet.
   b. the mind.
   c. the heart.

5. If you are trying to lose weight which of the following would be **taboo**?
   a. lettuce
   b. skim milk
   c. chocolate

6. If you were trying to **tempt** someone to break his diet, you would offer him
   a. salad.
   b. apple pie.
   c. a tuna sandwich.

Expand your understanding

 Complete each sentence by writing the correct vocabulary word in the space.

Vocabulary words		
rituals	token	taboo
avoid	psychological	tempt

1. Mattie tried to _____ her sister to miss her meeting by baking her favourite dessert.

2. We often _____ difficult tasks by putting them aside until tomorrow.

3. If a hockey player scores many goals in a game, he will have a _____ advantage next time he plays.

4. Anita ate a doughnut every morning; it was part of her daily _____.

5. Preparing food with unwashed hands is a _____ in restaurants.

6. Some pop machines take a _____ instead of cash.

"a lucky break"

It was "a lucky break" to meet Matt in the mall, since I needed a lift home.

When something happens that brings you good luck, you call it, "a lucky break."

Apply your understanding

 D Write sentences using the vocabulary words.

rituals _____

_____

avoid _____

_____

taboo _____

_____

tempt _____

_____

token _____

_____

psychological _____

_____

Extend your understanding

Our daily lives are filled with rituals. Rituals are small things we like to do every day in a certain way. For example, you may like to turn on the radio first thing in the morning to listen to the news. Your partner may want a cup of tea before getting out of bed. Our rituals reflect our likes and dislikes.

We also participate in rituals at work, in school, and at church. At work, you may always eat lunch with the same friends. You may even sit at the same table in the cafeteria. At school, you may listen to announcements before the start of classes. Religious services include many rituals such as singing hymns or saying prayers.

Doing the same thing over and over again is a comfort to us. Performing rituals with others outside the home helps us feel part of our community. Having our own rituals at home helps us form family ties.

 Think about the rituals you perform or participate in every day. Read the examples and then fill in the chart with your rituals.

	Home	Work	School	Church
Example	Having supper at the same time every night.	Having a cup of coffee before starting work.	Saying good morning to friends and teachers.	Making the sign of the cross when you enter the church.
Your ritual				

Crossword Puzzle 5

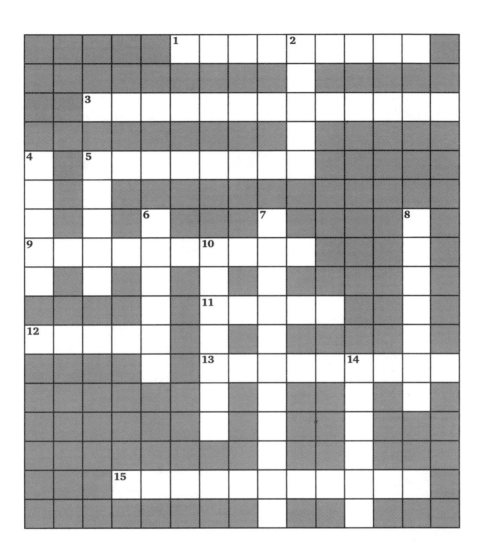

ACROSS

1. Threw away
3. To do with the mind
5. Obtained
9. Something scientists do
11. Large group of bees
12. Something that is forbidden
13. At the beginning
15. Destruction

DOWN

2. To keep away from
4. To mate and produce offspring
5. To adjust to new situations
6. Shaking
7. A synonym for residents
8. Activities that are regularly followed
10. Large and heavy
14. Weak, pale, and tired

Wordsearch 5

E	I	D	I	D	E	R	I	U	Q	C	A	R	D	A
X	N	I	C	N	O	I	P	N	M	D	O	S	E	Q
P	H	S	I	O	I	I	I	A	E	M	N	O	V	P
E	A	C	M	A	O	T	S	D	E	E	R	B	A	A
R	B	A	E	E	C	S	I	R	I	T	I	P	S	C
I	I	R	N	S	I	I	T	A	A	A	C	D	T	A
M	T	D	A	V	L	L	C	N	L	D	V	C	A	H
E	A	E	E	R	P	A	R	Y	E	L	L	O	T	D
N	N	D	A	T	H	I	U	O	T	M	Y	I	I	T
T	T	A	D	A	P	T	D	T	A	S	N	O	O	D
P	S	Y	C	H	O	L	O	G	I	C	A	L	N	S
C	M	D	N	S	M	O	M	Q	O	R	A	N	W	E
T	B	E	T	C	C	E	B	T	S	A	E	A	O	I
E	I	O	I	T	A	O	D	A	O	L	R	A	E	N
C	I	R	I	S	U	C	C	O	T	M	N	I	I	I

acquired

adapt

anemic

avoid

breed

devastation

discarded

experiment

inhabitants

initially

massive

psychological

ritual

swarm

taboo

tremor

Glossary

This glossary provides only one meaning for each word. This meaning reflects the way the word was taught in the passage.

A

abundant (ə-'bən-dənt) *adj.* (1) more than enough (2) plentiful

accumulate (ə-'kyü-myə-ˌlāt) *vb.* to collect or gather

acquire (ə-'kwīr) *vb.* to get or gain by one's own efforts

activate ('ak-tə-ˌvāt) *vb.* to make active or bring into action

adapt (ə-'dapt) *vb.* adjust to new situations

adaptable (ə-'dap-tə-bəl) *adj.* able to adjust to a new situation

aggressive (ə-'gres-iv) *adj.* showing a readiness to attack others

alert (ə-'lərt) *adj.* watchful and ready to take action

alter ('ôl-tər) *vb.* to change partly but not completely

ancient ('ān-shənt) *adj.* a time long ago

anemic (ə-'nē-mik) *adj.* (1) suffering from anemia (2) weak, pale, and tired

anxiety (ang-'zī-ət-ē) *n.* to feel worried or fearful about what might happen

avoid (ə-'vôid) *vb.* to keep away from

B

ban ('ban) *n.* an official order that forbids something

breed ('brēd) *vb.* to mate and produce offspring

bulge ('bəlj) *vb.* to swell or curve outward

bushy ('bûsh-ē) *adj.* thick and spreading out like a bush

C

chronic ('krän-ik) *adj.* lasting for a long time

clog ('kläg) *vb.* to make passage through difficult or impossible

cluster ('kləs-tər) *n.* a number of similar things growing or grouped together

commit (kə-'mit) *vb.* to do or perform, especially a crime or offense

conclusion (kən-'klü-zhən) *n.* final decision reached by reasoning

conservation (ˌkän-sər-'vā-shən) *n.* to preserve and protect

contradict (ˌkän-trə-'dikt) *vb.* (1) to be opposed to (2) to say the opposite of what someone else has said

convenient (kən-'vē-nyənt) *adj.* easy to do, use, or get to (2) causing little trouble or work

counteract (ˌkaûnt-ər-'akt) *vb.* (1) to act directly against (2) to undo the effect of with opposing action

D

debris (də-'brē) *n.* the junk or pieces left from something broken down or destroyed

defensive (di-'fen-siv) *n.* (1) self-protective attitude (2) ready to reject criticism

deplete (di-'plēt) *vb.* to make less by gradually using up

deposit (di-'päz-ət) *n.* a natural layers of sand, rocks, or minerals

deprivation (ˌdep-rə-'vā-shən) *n.* the absence, loss, or withholding of something needed

devastation ('dev-ə-'stā-shən) *n.* destruction

discard (dis-'kärd) *vb.* to throw away or get rid of as no longer valuable or useful

dispose (dis-'pōz) *vb.* to get rid of

E

enable (in-'ā-bəl) *vb.* (1) to make possible

ensure (in-'shûr) *vb.* to make sure, certain, or safe

eruption (i-'rəp-shən) *n.* a bursting forth

essential (i-'sen-chəl) *adj.* absolutely necessary

experiment (ik-'sper-ə-ˌment) *n.* a trial or test to find out about something

extinct (ik-'stingkt) *adj.* no longer existing

F

fashionable ('fash-ə-nə-bəl) *adj.* following the current style

filter ('fil-tər) *vb.* (1) to move or pass through slowly (2) to remove by passing through a filter

function ('fəngk-shən) *vb.* work; to serve a certain purpose

G

graze ('grāz) *vb.* to feed on grass

H

habitat ('hab-ə-ˌtat) *n.* the place where an animal or plant lives or grows in nature

hardy ('härd-ē) *adj.* able to put up with difficult conditions

harsh ('härsh) *adj.* causing physical discomfort

havoc ('hav-ək) *n.* great destruction and devastation

hectic ('hek-tik) *adj.* filled with excitement, activity, or confusion

hereditary (hə-'red-ə-ˌter-ē) *adj.* capable of being passed down from parents to children

hospitality (ˌhäs-pə-'tal-ət-ē) *n.* friendly and generous treatment of guests

I

indifference (in-'dif-ə-rəns) *n.* lack of interest

inhabitant (in-'hab-ət-ənt) *n.* a permanent resident

initially (in-'ish-əl-lē) *adv.* at the beginning

insulate ('in-sə-ˌlāt) *vb.* to cover or protect from heat, cold, or noise

interior (in-'tir-ē-ər) *adj.* (1) inland (2) far away from the coast or border

intrude (in-'trüd) *vb.* to come or enter without being invited

ironically (ī-rän-i-kə-lē) *adv.* a result that is directly opposite to what was expected

L

lava ('läv-ə) *n.* (1) melted rock coming from a volcano (2) lava that has cooled and hardened into rock

loom ('lüm) *vb.* to appear above or hang over, in a large or threatening shape

M

marine (mə-'rēn) *adj.* something to do with the sea

massive ('mas-iv) *adj.* very large, heavy, and solid

misconception (mis-ˌkän-'sep-shən) *n.* (1) a wrong idea (2) a misunderstanding

N

native ('nāt-iv) *adj.* born, grown, produced in a certain place or country

numb ('nəm) *adj.* lacking in feeling, especially caused from something cold

O

obsolete (ˌäb-sə-'lēt) *adj.* no longer in use

offense (ə-'fens) *n.* the act of breaking a law

offspring ('ôf-ˌspring) *n.* the young of a person, animal, or plant

optimistic (ˌäp-tə-'mis-tik) *adj.* feeling that everything will turn out well

overthrow (ˌō-vər-'thrō) *vb.* to cause the fall or end of

P

pace ('pās) *n.* rate of movement, progress, or development

passage ('pas-ij) *n.* a way through something

permanent ('pər-mə-nənt) *adj.* lasting or meant to last for a long time

plight ('plīt) *n.* a bad condition

potential (pə-'ten-chəl) *adj.* existing as a possibility

practice ('prak-təs) *vb.* repeated action in order to learn something well

Prairie ('preər-ē) *n.* a large area of flat or rolling grassland that is treeless

predict (pri-'dikt) *vb.* figure out and make a statement about the future

pressure ('presh-ər) *n.* a steady force applied to an area

prey ('prā) *vb.* to hunt and eat something

produce ('präd-ˌüs) *n.* fresh fruits and vegetables

psychological (ˌsī-kə-'läj-i-kəl) *adj.* of the mind

pump ('pəmp) *vb.* to push onward

puncture ('pəngk-chər) *n.* a hole or wound made by something pointed

R

rank ('rangk) *vb.* to take or have a certain position in a group

rare ('raər) *adj.* very uncommon

receding (ri-'sēd-ing) *vb.* going back or away

reduce (ri-'düs) *vb.* to make smaller or less

reef ('rēf) *n.* rocks or coral near the surface of the sea

reliable (ri-ˈlī-ə-bəl) *adj.* dependable and trustworthy

remote (ri-ˈmōt) *adj.* (1) far away (2) secluded

renewable (ri-ˈnü-ə-bəl) *adj.* able to be replaced or replenished

represent (ˌrep-ri-ˈzent) *vb.* to be a sign or symbol of

reprimand (ˈrep-rə-ˌmand) *vb.* to criticize a person severely

resistant (ri-ˈzis-tənt) *adj.* incapable of being affected

restore (ri-ˈstōr) *vb.* to put or bring back to an earlier or original state

risk factor (ˈrisk ˈfak-tər) *n.* a circumstance or condition that increases a specific risk

ritual (ˈrich-ə-wəl) *n.* a procedure regularly followed

rotate (ˈrō-ˌtāt) *vb.* to turn around on an axis or centre

S

sag (ˈsag) *vb.* to hang down loosely below the right level

significant (sig-ˈnif-i-kənt) *adj.* important and having a special meaning

solitary (ˈsäl-ə-ˌter-ē) *adj.* growing or living alone

specialties (ˈspesh-əl-tēs) *n.* a product of a special kind

staple (ˈstā-pəl) *n.* the main or chief part of something

strenuous (ˈstren-yə-wəs) *adj.* requiring great effort or energy

swept (ˈswept) *vb.* moved over or across quickly with force or destruction

T

taboo (tə-ˈbü) *n.* prohibited or forbidden by tradition

tempt (ˈtempt) *vb.* to try to persuade someone to do a wrong or forbidden thing

tense (ˈtens) *adj.* feeling or showing nervous tension

testosterone (te-ˈstäs-tə-ˌrōn) *n.* a male hormone

token (ˈtō-kən) *n.* (1) keepsake or souvenir (2) something of sentimental value

transport (ˈtrans-ˌpōrt) *vb.* to carry from one place to another

tremor (ˈtrem-ər) *n.* shaking movements

trend (ˈtrend) *n.* (1) current style. (2) general direction and tendency

trigger (ˈtrig-ər) *v.* an event that causes a reaction

U

unique (yû-ˈnēk) *adj.* (1) being the only one of its kind (2) very unusual

universal (ˌyü-nə-ˈvər-səl) *adj.* present or happening everywhere

V

venom (ˈven-əm) *n.* poison made by an animal and passed to a victim by a bite or sting

versatile (ˈvər-sət-l) *adj.* able to do many different kinds of things

vibrate (ˈvī-ˌbrāt) *vb.* to move rapidly back and forth

Answer Key

Lesson 1 Understanding Stress

A 1.b; 2.a; 3.b; 4.c; 5.a; 6.a

B 1.b; 2.b; 3.b; 4.b; 5.c; 6.b

C conclusion; pump; practice; optimistic; tense; anxiety

E reappear – to appear again; regain – to get something back; refund – to pay back money; refill – to fill something again; replace – to put something back in its place; recall – to remember; rebuild – to build again

Lesson 2 The Black Widow Spider

A 1.c; 2.b; 3.a; 4.b; 5.b; 6.c

B 1.b; 2.b; 3.b; 4.b; 5.a; 6.b

C debris; numb; puncture; venom; resistant; preys

E waste; garbage; rubbish; rubble; remains; fragments
1. preys; 2. venom; 3. resistant; 4. puncture; 5. numb

Lesson 3 Mount St. Helens

A 1.a; 2.c; 3.c; 4.a; 5.b; 6.b

B 1.b; 2.c; 3.b; 4.a; 5.b; 6.c

C pressure; eruption; lava; triggered; swept; bulged

E Some examples of homophones:
bored/board; break/brake; find/fined; flower/flour; hair/hare; heal/heel; maid/made; new/knew; plain/plane; pear/pair; sea/see; stairs/stares; waste/waist

Lesson 4 Bread

A 1.b; 2.a; 3.b; 4.c; 5.a; 6.c

B 1.b; 2.b; 3.b; 4.a; 5.b; 6.a

C overthrow; Prairies; staple; hospitality; significant; ancient

E jellyfish – a sea animal that looks like jelly; newspaper – a daily or weekly paper about the news; daylight – natural light during the day; timetable – a list showing times; handmade – something made by hand; underground – below the ground

Lesson 5 Shift Work

A 1.b; 2.b; 3.a; 4.c; 5.c; 6.a

B 1.b; 2.c; 3.a; 4.b; 5.b; 6.a

C function; activates; alert; alter; restores; essential

E Answers may vary.

Lesson 6 Tigers in Trouble

A 1.a; 2.c; 3.b; 4.a; 5.a; 6.c

B 1.c; 2.c; 3.a; 4.a; 5.b; 6.b

C ban; conservation; extinct; predicted; plight; habitat

E 1. F; 2. T; 3. F

Lesson 7 Oil Spill at Sea

A 1.c; 2.c; 3.a; 4.b; 5.a; 6.c

B 1.a; 2.b; 3.b; 4.c; 5.b; 6.c

C reduce; insulate; transport; marine; reef; remote

E Answers may vary.

Lesson 8 Body Language

A 1.b; 2.a; 3.a; 4.c; 5.c; 6.c

B 1.b; 2.a; 3.b; 4.c; 5.b; 6.a

C reprimanded; universal; unique; contradicts; indifference; defensive

E 1. uniform; 2.university; 3. united; 4. unicorns; 5. union

Lesson 9 The Problem with Snoring

A 1.a; 2.a; 3.b; 4.b; 5.c; 6.a

B 1.b; 2.a; 3.b; 4.a; 5.c; 6.b

C sag; deprivation; chronic; risk factors; passage; vibrate

E Answers may vary.

Lesson 10 Black Bears

A 1.c; 2.b; 3.a; 4.c; 5.a; 6.c

B 1.b; 2.b; 3.a; 4.c; 5.a; 6.b

C enabled; intrude; adaptable; versatile; solitary; misconception

E Answers may vary.

Lesson 11 Antarctica

A 1.a; 2.c; 3.b; 4.c; 5.a; 6c

B 1. c; 2.a; 3.b; 4.b; 5.b; 6.c

C interior; permanent; abundant; dispose; harsh; hardy

E 1. outside; 2. outdoors; 3.exhale; 4. outward; 5. output

Lesson 12 The Slow Food Movement

A 1.b; 2.a; 3.c; 4.a; 5.c; 6.b

B 1.a; 2.c; 3.b; 4.c; 5.b; 6.b

C specialties; pace; convenient; produce; counteract; hectic

E 1. fruits and vegtables; 2. to bring forth or yield; 3. to create; 4. to bring forth or yield; 5. make; 6. make

Lesson 13 Hair Loss

A 1.c; 2.a; 3.c; 4.b; 5.a; 6.b

B 1.c; 2.c; 3.b; 4.c; 5.c; 6.a

C receding; testosterone; reliable; bushy; rare; hereditary

E Answers may vary.

Lesson 14 Zebra Mussels
A 1.c; 2.c; 3.a; 4.b; 5.a; 6.b
B 1.b; 2.b; 3.a; 4.c; 5.c; 6.a
C filter; native; block; accumulate; havoc; clusters
E 1.c; 2.a; 3.b

Lesson 15 Wind Power
A 1.b; 2.a; 3.b; 4.c; 5.c; 6.a
B 1.b; 2.a; 3.b; 4.b; 5.c; 6.b
C depleted; rotate; graze; renewable; potential; obsolete
E non-profit; nonfiction; nontoxic; non-stop; non-dairy

Lesson 16 Tattoos
A 1.b; 2.a; 3.c; 4.b; 5.a; 6.c
B 1.b; 2.b; 3.a; 4.a; 5.b; 6.c
C committed; represented; trend; rank; fashionable; offense
E Answers may vary.

Lesson 17 Donating Blood
A 1.c; 2.b; 3.a; 4.b; 5.c; 6.a
B 1.a; 2.b; 3.c; 4.b; 5.c; 6.b
C acquired; anemic; ensure; strenuous; discarded; initially
E Answers may vary.

Lesson 18 Killer Bees
A 1.a; 2.b; 3.a; 4.a; 5.b; 6.c
B 1.b; 2.b; 3.b; 4.a; 5.c; 6.a
C offspring; ironically; breed; experiment; adapt; aggressive
E 1. S; 2. P; 3. S; 4. S; 5. P; 6. S; 7. P; 8. S; 9. P; 10. P

Lesson 19 The Mountain that Walks
A 1.b; 2.c; 3.b; 4.a; 5.b; 6.c
B 1.a; 2.a; 3.c; 4.a; 5.b; 6.c
C loomed; inhabitants; massive; tremors; deposits; devastation
E Answers may vary.

Lesson 20 Superstitions
A 1.a; 2.c; 3.a; 4.c; 5.b; 6.b
B 1.a; 2.c; 3.a; 4.b; 5.c; 6.b
C tempt; avoid; psychological; ritual; taboo; token
E Answers may vary.

Crossword Puzzles Answers

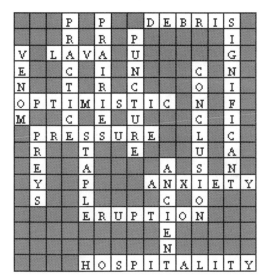

Crossword Puzzle 1

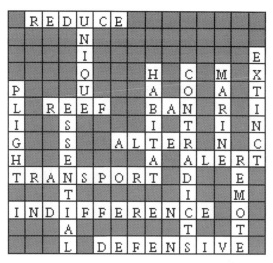

Crossword Puzzle 2

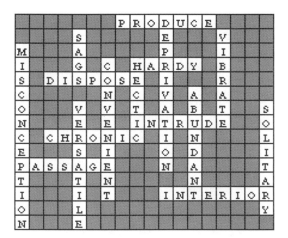

Crossword Puzzle 3

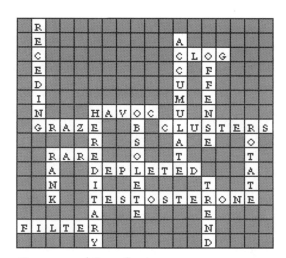

Crossword Puzzle 4

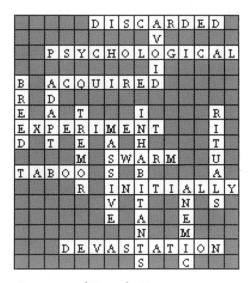

Crossword Puzzle 5

Wordsearch Answers

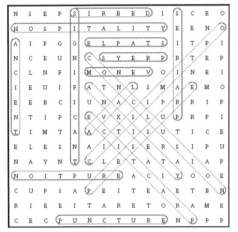

Wordsearch 1

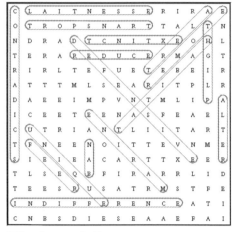

Wordsearch 2

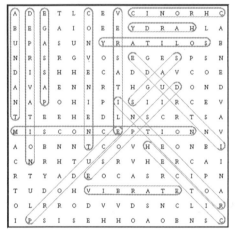

Wordsearch 3

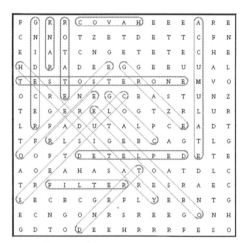

Wordsearch 4

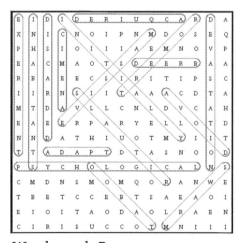

Wordsearch 5